WICCA FOR MEN

WICCA FOR MEN

A Handbook for
Male Pagans Seeking a
Spiritual Path

A. J. DREW

A CITADEL PRESS BOOK
Published by Carol Publishing Group

Copyright © 1998 A. J. Drew

A Citadel Press Book
Published by Carol Publishing Group
Citadel Press is a registered trademark of Carol Communications, Inc.

Editorial, sales and distribution, rights and permissions inquiries should be addressed to Carol Publishing Group, 120 Enterprise Avenue, Secaucus, N.J. 07094

In Canada: Canadian Manda Group, One Atlantic Avenue, Suite 105, Toronto, Ontario M6K 3E7

Carol Publishing Group books may be purchased in bulk at special discounts for sales promotion, fund-raising, or educational purposes. Special editions can be created to specifications. For details, contact Special Sales Department, 120 Enterprise Avenue, Secaucus, N.J. 07094.

Manufactured in the United States of America
10 9 8 7 6 5 4 3 2 1

Library of Congress Cataloging-in-Publication Data

Drew, A. J.
    Wicca for men : a handbook for male pagans seeking a spiritual
path / by A. J. Drew.
        p.   cm.
    "A Citadel Press book."
    Includes bibliographical references.
    ISBN 0-8065-2023-X (pbk.)
    1. Witchcraft.   I. Title.
BF1571.5.M45D74   1998
299—dc21   98-29048
                                                                 CIP

For my father, my son, and my sister
and the time we have not had together.

Look, Mom, no hands!

Contents

Acknowledgments

Thanks to Stephen Sowers (the Mad Potter) for his assistance even when I was going insane. Thanks to Susan Sowers for not killing Stephen while he was helping me. A great deal of thanks to Holly Hahn and Jennifer Hunt (Muddy) for insights and for taking time to help. I thank Patricia Telesco for lighting the fire that this book has become, Sirona Knight for blowing on the coals, and Brian Ryman for stoking it.

All diagrams are courtesy of Brian Ryman.

Introduction

"Double, double toil and trouble," three old hags chant as they stir the contents of a large black cauldron, which may include the breath of a baby and perhaps an adder's tongue or two. Is this a typical night for a Witch? Well, not really. Last night I had pizza and beer.

During the past two thousand years, Witchcraft has received a lot of bad publicity. There have been many ridiculous perceptions of what a Witch looks like and what a Witch does. The haggard-looking green-skinned old woman with warts and a long nose surfaces every October. The blood-thirsty she devil seeking a virgin child for her next sacrifice can often be found on late night television. With better understanding and the rapid growth of the modern Witchcraft movement, many of these stereotypes have fallen away. The fact that modern Witchcraft is a nature-oriented religion with ties to ancient fertility religions has almost become common knowledge. Books on the subject are available in most libraries and mainstream bookstores. Television news and talk shows have been dedicated to the subject. Articles often appear in local and national newspapers. But with the death of the old misconceptions, new ones have arisen.

One of the more recent misconceptions about Witchcraft, often call Wicca, is that all present day Wiccans are lesbians. Surprise! Not only are the majority of Wiccans *not* lesbians, many of us are not female. The word *Wicca* is actually on Old English term which means "male Witch." The modern Witchcraft movement is as diverse as any other segment of the larger community. We are male and female, straight and gay, white and black—and a rainbow of shades in between. United by a few simple but deeply felt beliefs, our diversity is our strength. Modern Witchcraft is a living and growing expression of these beliefs, which are often so close to the heart that it is hard for a practitioner of Wicca to believe that anyone, when given the choice, would choose another spiritual path.

However, Wicca is not the best religious choice for every person. Most Wiccans realize this and make an extra effort not to proselytize. Wicca makes room for paradoxes, believing seemingly opposite religious structures can both be right. Wicca does not claim that any one religion is better than the next. What is right for one person is not necessarily right for another person.

Although diverse, Wicca is a religion defined by many regulatory groups within the U.S. government. Many Wiccan churches have achieved tax-exempt status with the Internal Revenue Service. Each of the fifty states grants ministry licenses to Wiccan clergy. As a soldier, my dogs tags listed Wicca as my religious preference. There are numerous other ways in which Wicca has been legally recognized as a religion.

Wicca is a joy-filled, nature-based religion that honors fertility and the life force. We choose to see the Creator as the marriage or union of male and female, God and Goddess, because that is how we create life. Although this way of viewing the Creator is ancient, it has been suppressed in common Western knowledge for almost two millennia. Most Westerners simply accept what their parents have taught them, that the Creator is male. This is clearly evident in such places as the Lord's Prayer: "Our *Father* who art in heaven . . ." Even when this programming has not been direct, it is present. In a more passive form, the belief that the Creator is wholly male is built into our language. "He" is the most common pronoun used to refer to the Creator. In prayer, visualization, and other religious practices, Wiccans often call on either God or Goddess individually, but try to always be aware that neither God nor Goddess is Creator without the other.

This book is not exclusively for men. It carries the title because many of the issues I address are male issues. As one of the goals of the feminist movements is to explain the female condition to males, one of the goals of this book is to explain the condition of male Wiccans to female Wiccans. After all, there can be no day without night, nor warmth without cold; there can be no female without male.

Unfortunately, after so many years of being in a male-dominated society, the idea that the Creator might not be wholly male is such a well-received philosophy that the balance which Wicca seeks has become jeopardized. Many who have adopted the tenants of this joyous religion have swung all the way to the Goddess side of the forum, ignoring the male component almost completely. For evidence of this, sneeze in a room full of Wiccans and see how many respond with "God bless you." A glance at my shop's mailing list will reveal that the majority of Wiccans are female. It seems odd that Wiccans are predominantly female, as the religion itself is based on the praise of life in its equal male and female attributes. Neither the male nor the female is praised above the other. It would seem then, that Wicca should attract men and women in equal numbers.

There is absolutely no room for sexism within the Wiccan community, nor is there room for racism. Such prejudices are born of ignorance and have no place in a religion that has been called "the Craft of the Wise." Although when Wicca was originally introduced it drew primarily on Celtic lore, today it is free to draw on the traditions of many cultures. During drum circles to raise energy, African jimbeys are the preferred drum, beating out the traditional Celtic bodhran by at least ten to one. Dancing seems to most resemble what one would expect to find in the Middle East, and chants combine the names of deities from around the world.

If you are Wiccan or a member of another Pagan denomination, chances are you may have already accepted the fact that the natural way to view the Creator is as a union of male and female. Unfortunately, in your rebellion against the typical patriarchal rhetoric, you may have neglected more than a full half of the joy and love that your Creator has for you, the half that is God.

I wrote this book because I felt it was needed by both the Wiccan community and the Western mind-set. More than any other aspiration, I hope to cause people to think, especially for themselves.

Wicca for Men outlines the basics of Creation's Covenant, a tradition (denomination) of Wicca. Its name reflects the exact meaning behind our commitment—a covenant is a pact or promise. This tradition is our pact or promise with Creation. Unlike many other traditions, we make absolutely no claim that our path can be followed all the way back to a pre-Christian era. We are a modern tradition, considering ourselves to be very progressive and appreciative of today's technology. You can even find us on the World Wide Web at www.neopagan.com/creation

Nowhere in this work will you find it said that men are superior. The rituals contained herein are designed to enforce the balance in the psyche while manifesting a positive impact on our social condition. Whether you are a long-practicing Wiccan or novice, this book will show you new ways of expressing what you already know: that life is joyous and should be celebrated joyously. This is Wicca as it should be, neither male nor female dominated. It is Wicca as a positive, life-affirming, truly spiritual religion that helps its members to grow in harmony with the earth and with each other.

WICCA FOR MEN

I

The Old Religion

The Birth of the Old Religions

Placing an exact date on the birth of Witchcraft is impossible because the word means different things to different people, but it is not the exact date that is important. Most important are the reasons for and applications of the ideas that Witchcraft embraces. I choose to start my story at the dawn of life, because it is life that Witchcraft honors.

Creation's Covenant teaches that before there was life on this planet, lightning struck the ocean. From this event came the building blocks of what would later become life. In symbolic terms, the ocean is the womb of the Goddess, and the lightning is the phallus of the God. This was the first Great Rite, the holiest of rituals, the union of male and female. It was the very act of Creation.

Commonly accepted science says that millions of years later, our ancestors climbed out of the proverbial tree and that about one hundred thousand years ago, modern man, or *Homo sapiens*, took his first steps. While I have been told

I look like the missing link, I was not there. However, I theorize that as *Homo sapiens* literally means "man having sense," it was probably not long before humanity used that sense to first question the nature of creation.

At the early stages of humanity, we could not have understood the cause-and-effect relationship between sex and pregnancy. The Creator must have been viewed as wholly female because it was only the female who was visually responsible for creating life. Archaeological finds support this view with examples of the veneration of the female and, in particular, her reproductive and nurturing attributes. Wide hips and huge breasts were typical of early female deity figures. This veneration is evidenced by archaeological finds such as the Venus or Earth Mother of Willendorf, a 4⅛" limestone statue discovered in Austria that has been dated to 25,000 B.C.E., and the Earth Mother of Laussel, a limestone relief discovered in France, that has been dated to 20,000 B.C.E., as well as many others.

Because nature delegated the duty of pregnancy to the female, by default other duties fell to the male. One of these duties was hunting. With hunting came the need for a deity of the hunt. To better associate this deity to the animals being hunted, many of the animals' attributes were given to this deity, such as horns, hoofs, and sometimes a tail. Because those hunting were predominantly male, the god of the hunt took a male form. Without modern weapons, hunting was extremely dangerous and the hunting party would often return with less men than it started with. Thus the god of the hunt also became the god of sacrifice and death. As he became the bridge between men and other animals, he also became the bridge between life and death. He was both the proud hunter and the hunted, sacrificing himself for the good of the tribe.

The images of Goddess as creator (mother) and God as provider (father) formed the first concepts of a dual deity and these gender roles are still played to an extent today.

The Maturation of the Old Religions

The revelation that men play an integral part in creating life was responsible for expanding the original view of God. Instead of seeing the male half of the deity as provider alone, he became consort, lover, and father. The idea of a fertility god was born. As humanity expanded its knowledge and domain, the views of deity also expanded. As race and regional attributes developed, the God and Goddess changed to better relate to the people who praised them. Where humanity was dark of skin, God and Goddess were often dark of skin: where light in complexion, so were God and Goddess.

In regions where women hunted, the huntress was brought into one aspect of Goddess. In areas where agriculture was more important than hunting, God and Goddess were both linked to vegetation. The Gods and Goddesses of nature became so entrenched in the European mind-set that they exist to this day. In England, references to Pagan God-forms like Jack of the Wood or the Green Man are as common as Mother Nature is in the United States.

The many concepts of deity differed from region to region, changing as the needs for survival in different climates and societies changed. When tribes migrated and lost contact with each other, spiritual diversities increased. Eventually, the spiritual paths diverged enough that separate religions became evident. However, each religion retained common elements: each was nature-based and

applicable to the society in which the religion was practiced, and each served the needs of its people.

Throughout much of this time, there was little difference
between magick, science, and religion. Because divinity was
thought to be a function of nature, it was only common
sense that those who explained nature would be those who
explained the Gods. Little difference was seen between religion and science, priest and scientist, astrology and astron-
omy, prayer and magick. When the sick visited a healer,
both medicine and prayer would be administered.

This is where humanity's almost universal views of the
Gods and Goddesses remained for many eons. Spirituality
was based in the sensible and natural concept of deity in
our image, both male and female, each, like us, having
many facets and personality traits. As the roles of men and
women changed, so did the roles of God and Goddess.

The Death of Old Religions

For about 98,400 years—from the beginnings of humanity
(about 98,000 B.C.E.) until the creation of the New Testa-
ment in the fifth century C.E.—there was no central religious authority; no one religion could satisfy the needs of
drastically different people. Throughout time, many wars
have been fought between opposing religions, but none
came close to the atrocities and crimes against humanity as
was done in the name of Christianity.

The death of the old religions can be directly associated
with the birth of Christianity. Because Christianity is a
supernatural religion, its introduction was not met fondly
by the country folk of the time. These people worshiped
Gods and Goddesses who had a direct impact on the harvest, the hunt, and other life-giving and -sustaining events.

The old religions had evolved alongside their strifes and accomplishments. Convincing them to give up the old ways in favor of the latest fad was not easy—especially when the rewards of the new religion would only be seen upon one's death, while the rewards of the old religion were seen in every harvest and every birth. Instead, Christianity found its first home in the cities. There, like fashion or plague, it spread quickly through human contact.

Christianity's teachings, that there was one completely male creator who was all good and who was opposed by Satan, another male figure—yet not a deity—who was completely evil, must have seemed completely alien to the country folk of that time. Because the reality of nature could never be simplified into good and evil, white and black, the concept of a natural deity could not be simplified in that way.

Originally the word *pagan* meant "country dweller" and had no religious implications. The pre-Christian use of the word by city dwellers would be similar to the use of the words "hick" or "hillbilly" today. At the point where the cities were predominantly Christian and the countryside predominantly non-Christian, the word came to describe one who was other than Christian.

But Christianity was not content to be just one of many religions, it wanted to be the *only* religion. At first, this was done with less than lethal force. To strengthen the Church's views among the city folk, they distorted Pagan customs and made them seem as though evil. (Ironically, some of those customs have become Christian traditions, such as the decorating of a tree at Yule time.) Because many of the Pagan gods of the hunt were horned, the Church associated them with the Christian Satan. Fertility religions were thought wholly Satanic because the new Church believed sex was sinful.

One of the biggest differences was how women were perceived. Prior to Christian rule, women were venerated as the source of life. This new ideology saw women as the source of original sin. Because women and Witchcraft were both linked to sin, the association between women and Witchcraft was forged. Because the Church state was male-dominated, it propagated the idea that the old religions were female-dominated in order to strengthen their premise that the old religions were evil.

There are many other examples of the slanders, but probably the most absurd was the Church's insistence that Pagans conducted rituals to blight the harvest. When one considers the fact that those responsible for the rites were the ones who would directly benefit or suffer based on the harvest, it's obvious how ridiculous such an idea was.

Because the country dwellers, or Pagans, were viewed as anti-Christian, their ways were viewed as a threat. However, the Pagans had lived off the land and they possessed knowledge of plants and herbs, the only medicines of the time. So when the Church denounced Pagan practices, health care fell into decline as people stopped believing in the healing power of nature and more in the "healing power" of the Church. Almost anything that could not be found in the Church's holy book was considered evil. Quality of living plummeted.

Also changed by the church was the meaning of the word *Witan*. Originally, the Witan were the advisors to kings and leaders. They were often an eclectic lot, composed of many traditions and disciplines. Although the roots of the word *Witch* are widely disputed, I believe it was invented by the Church as a slur of the word Witan.

While the misinformation campaign did help the Church create public support for their policy of eliminating what they saw as a threat, it did not do much to dissuade the common folk from their old practices. Stronger steps were initiated. Pope Gregory the Great ordered the destruction of the old Pagan temples and the construction of Christian churches in their places. Many of the artisans who were chosen to build these new churches were themselves devoted to the old Gods and Goddesses, and therefore, many of the first Christian churches were built with images of the old Gods and Goddesses incorporated into their structure.

By the fifteenth century, the Church realized their efforts to convert non-Christians might not have been entirely success-ful. The old religions were deeply rooted. To solve this pesky little problem, the church deemed that anyone non-Christian and unwilling to convert must be tortured and killed. The cry of the Church became "convert or die!" This is clearly evi-denced by the *Malleus Maleficarum* (commonly called the "Witches Hammer") an official publication of the Roman Catholic church, put out around 1484. With the endorse-ment of Pope Innocent VIII, this book sought to end the one thousand years of Christian abuse against the old reli-gions. It did just that, by serving as the instrument which would be used to attempt to kill not only all remaining Pagans but many Christians and Jews as well.

The *Malleus Maleficarum* was indiscriminant in who should be tortured and killed. Not only were Witches and sympathizers targeted, but anyone who did not believe in the existence of Witches was also at risk. The Witch hunters destroyed entire villages when they suspected one or two of the villagers were witches. There was little concern for whether those being slaughtered were actually Witches. Indeed, many were not.

Under Catholic law, the Church could seize land and property owned by anyone found guilty of Witchcraft or anyone practicing the old religions. Oftentimes, the accused were forced to pay for their own trial and incarceration.

The accusations grew, born partly out of paranoia, partly out of greed, and partly out of fear. Accusations became a political tool and a method of removing a rival or changing an undesired situation. For example, the Church rarely allowed divorce. If a husband became unhappy with his wife, he could simply accuse her of Witchcraft. Unfortunately for the wife, one of the only ways she could be found innocent was by sinking when bound and thrown into a body of water. The charges against her would be dismissed posthumously, and her husband would be rid of her. If she floated, however, it was said that the devil was lifting her and she would be burned at the stake. Either way her husband would be free of her.

The *Malleus Maleficarum* gave the impression that Satan lurked around every corner. In fear, Christians turned to the Church for protection from the perceived enemy. In response to the terror, the Church set about stomping out not only those who opposed its views, but those who peacefully ignored its teachings. Anything that the church opposed was labeled Witchcraft or Satanism or heresy. Although these labels are clearly distinct, they were eventually indiscriminately lumped together in the group with science, magick, herbalism, midwifery—and anything else the Church opposed.

Even those with similar religious views to the church were labeled heretics. An excellent example of such persecution is found in one of the most popular methods with which to prove Witchcraft. It was said that a Witch could not recite the Lord's Prayer properly. When a Witch was being accused this was an easy way to prove guilt as the two churches taught distinctly different versions of the prayer. Even the ten commandments differed from denomination to denomination. Reviewing the names of European people put to death on the charge of Witchcraft, it is interesting to note how many names sound Jewish. Ironically, if the story of Jesus is true, he was put to death on charges very similar to those waged against condemned heretics and Witches.

Knowing that discovery meant torture and death, the few who were faithful to the old religions went into hiding. Where once an entire village would mark the Pagan celebrations together, smaller groups formed to ensure secrecy. Where rites were commonly celebrated in the full light of day, practitioners took to hiding their rites under the cover of darkness. Where bright festive colors were worn to commemorate seasonal changes, black and dark colors, which blend into the night, became the norm. Because the sun and moon have gendered energies, the need to choose moonlight (female) over sunlight (male) further associated Witchcraft with the female.

The effects of Christianity establishing itself as the path to follow for the times were devastating. In addition to the witch-hunts, the Inquisition, Crusades, and infighting between different denominations of Christianity, consider the loss of life due to the teachings of the Church. The plagues that struck Europe in the Middle Ages and killed more than half the population can be attributed to the parasites carried by rats. Without the Church's widespread slaughter of cats—believing they were linked to Witchcraft—the rat population would have been kept in check and the casualties perhaps lessened.

By the sixteenth century, almost all signs of the old religion were gone. This is evidenced by the fact that when King Edward VI repealed the English laws against Witchcraft in 1547, there was not a rushing forth of Pagans to set the record straight. In 1563, shortly after his death, the laws were reinstated. In 1604, King James I enacted a new series anti-Witchcraft laws, but these were nullified when the majority of the English anti-Witchcraft laws were again repealed in 1736 by King George II and again there were not hordes of Pagans emerging from hiding. In England, from 1736 to present time, the only active laws pertaining to Witchcraft were enacted as antifraud laws, but still there are no highly visible signs of Witchcraft being widely practiced as a fertility religion.

Many Pagan customs, however, have refused to be forgotten. Some have found their way into the culture of the Church, in the form of Christmas trees and Easter eggs. Others became myths and fairy tales, allowed to continue because they seemed merely for the amusement of children. (Many old Pagan Gods and Goddesses became Christian saints such as the Pagan Goddess Brigid becoming St. Brigit, the Pagan God Lugh becoming St. Michael, and the Pagan God Mabon becoming St Andrew.) The seeds of Paganism lay scattered, waiting for a time of religious tolerance when they could once again be reassembled. But openly, the Pagan religions had perished.

2

Wicca: The New "Old Religion"

The Birth of Wicca

Little is known about the practice of Witchcraft between the sixteenth century and the middle of the twentieth century. If there were practicing Witches, they were well hidden. It wasn't until 1921 that the hysterical rantings of the Church about Witchcraft were really challenged. In that year, Witchcraft was examined by Dr. Margaret Murrary, an eminent anthropologist and teacher at University College in London, who published her views in *The Witch Cult in Western Europe*, and then expanded upon them in a second book, *The God of the Witches*, in 1931.

Murray claimed that Witchcraft was actually a pre-Christian fertility religion. She drew a line between the magick and religion of Witchcraft by calling the magick aspect "operational Witchcraft" and the religious aspect "ritual Witchcraft." As these terms can become confusing, I will continue to use the term *Witchcraft* for religion, but will use the word "*spellcraft*" to refer to operational Witchcraft.

Although the majority of the English anti-Witchcraft laws were repealed in 1736, it wasn't until 1951 that all were removed from the official record. Many of these last few laws dealt specifically with fraud.

One of the first positive books published on the subject was *Witchcraft Today* (1954) by Gerald Gardner, an English Witch. Although there is great debate as to exactly how far his particular denomination of Witchcraft can be traced, there can be no doubt that he was one of the first people to make the practice of Witchcraft widely available.

Mr. Gardner supported many of Dr. Murray's theories. His book confirmed that not only had Witchcraft been a pre-Christian fertility religion, but revealed the fact it still is. He knew this because he claimed that he himself was a Witch— more specifically, a Wiccan. Mr. Gardner became the first person to use the word *Wicca* to describe modern Witchcraft, and the word *Wiccan* to describe a modern Witch.

Unlike Dr. Murray, Mr. Gardner was a press grabber. His "coming out of the broom closet" quickly became the subject of newspaper headlines. Many others soon came forward and claimed to be associated with Witchcraft groups (covens). Some even claimed their Witchcraft lineage had been perpetuated in secret from a time before the Middle Ages.

Raymond Buckland was initiated by Mr. Gardner's High Priestess about a year before Mr. Gardner died. He later moved to the United States, where he introduced the Gardnerian Tradition of Wicca (named after its founder Mr. Gardner) in the early 1960s. By proxy, Gardner became responsible for much of the Witchcraft revival in the United States. In 1971, Buckland's book *Witchcraft From the Inside* made the revival even more available in the United States. In 1973, Mr. Buckland announced the formation of his own tradition, Seax Wica (note the single 'c'). I tend to think Mr. Buckland was attempting to use the spelling difference to further distance Seax Wica from Gardnerian Wicca. It was as if Mr. Gardner had created the seed and Mr. Buckland sowed it in fertile land. In the United States, where religious freedom is guaranteed by the Bill of Rights, the Craft flourished.

Back in Europe, the modern Witchcraft movement also continued to grow. In the late 1960s and early '70s, the English press took an interest in a Witch by the name of Alex Sanders, who established Alexandrian Wicca in England. Mr. Sanders claimed his lineage was separate from the Gardnerian tradition, and that he had been initiated by his grandmother. Although she herself was a Witch, the tradition had skipped his parents. Reportedly, it would have missed him as well if it were not for him catching his grandmother practicing and receiving an instant initiation from her in exchange for his silence. The Alexandrian tradition is very similar to the Gardnerian tradition, although the Alexandrian tradition pays a little more attention to ceremonial magick. Just as Mr. Buckland nurtured the Gardnerian tradition, Janet and Stewart Farrar nurtured the Alexandrian tradition with the publication of numerous books.

The news that there was an alternative to the prevailing Western religions generated a great deal of interest in Witchcraft. In the United States, the introduction of Wicca as a spiritual choice coincided almost perfectly with other revolutions taking place. Women's rights were at the top of the list of demands for social reform. The teachings of modern Witchcraft showed that women were the equals of men. Also, the sexual revolution was in full swing. Men and women were casting away the Church's teachings that sex was for procreation only, while modern Witchcraft taught that all acts of love were sacred. After more than a thousand years of oppression, the human spirit was reawakening and modern Witchcraft was there to embrace it.

Although Mr. Gardner, Mr. Sanders, and others offered very similar accounts of how they felt Wicca should be practiced, many paths were taken that lead from those central starting points. Dianic Wicca, started by Morgan McFarland, follows many of the same guidelines as Gardnerian and Alexandrian Wicca, but places an even larger emphasis on the Goddess. So-called Dianic Feminist Witchcraft is similar to and often confused with Dianic Wicca, except that Dianic Feminist Witchcraft tends to focus on Goddess to the point of being monotheistic. Faerie Wicca (as founded in Arizona in 1979), which is often confused with Faery Wicca, a tradition that focuses on Celtic lore, appears to be a homosexual tradition which forms predominantly gay covens. Many, many other traditions have been formed. Some groups choose to refer to themselves as traditional. These groups place most of their focus on legends and folkways rather than on the recent writings. Others groups and individual Witches call themselves eclectic Witches. These Witches take aspects and practices from many different traditions and combine them to suit their own needs.

The Maturation of Wicca

Perhaps the most influential factor in the maturation of Wicca came with the introduction of Scott Cunningham's book, *Wicca: A Guide for the Solitary Practitioner*, in 1988. This book gave accreditation to Wiccans who practice without a coven or group. The old belief was that it takes a Witch to create a Witch, usually through an initiation ritual performed by a coven. This new belief taught that being Wiccan was a matter of the heart and that one could become Wiccan through a rite of self-dedication. This shift in thinking allowed Wicca to grow at an incredible rate. Today, many believe Wicca to be the single fastest growing religion in the United States.

As one who lives immersed in the modern Pagan community, I have been fortunate enough to view the changes firsthand. Where once the community insisted there was a clear connection between the Pagans of today and the Pagans of old, the word Neo-Pagan has come to denote the four or five hundred year break in continuity. Where once the focus was on tradition and returning to the ways of the early Pagans, today's Neo-Pagans are shifting the focus to individuality and discovering new ways to incorporate beliefs that transcend the ages.

As I write this, we are almost a half century from the time the word *wicca* came to be used as a term for modern Witchcraft. There is still a lingering debate over the origins of the word. Some claim it comes from the word *wicce* (also *wicee* and *wiccee*) which means "to bend." Those who subscribe to this belief support their opinion with the legend of the willow. While the Druids believed that the oak was the strongest tree, the Wiccans realized that the willow, because of its ability to bend, would survive a wind that would topple the oak. This story expresses a common Wiccan belief that the ability to bend is a strength. The word wicca is also said to be related to the ability to bend energy.

Wicca has also been said to mean "craft of the wise," or that perhaps it was derived from the term *Witan*, a word given to counselors of English kings during Pagan times. The Witan were an eclectic group, often leaders from many different disciplines. This is a nice idea. With the majority of today's Wiccans practicing as solitaries, this etymology accurately reflects the modern expression of the ancient ways. You see, as the Witan of old were often leaders of their particular belief systems, modern Wiccans are their

own leader, especially so when practicing as a solitary practitioner. Each Wiccan has the ability to be his or her own
priest or priestess.

Unfortunately, while these theories are both politically
correct and applicable, it is likely that they are both wrong.
The etymology of the word Witch can rage on forever, but
the original meaning of the word Wicca is fairly clear.
While the majority of people who call themselves Wiccan
are female, the word Wicca is the masculine form of the
word Witch. The feminine form of the word is Wicce. Yes,
Wicca was a term used to describe a male Witch. To verify
this, look up the word Witch in a dictionary that predates
the Wiccan movement. Why Mr. Gardner chose the word
Wicca remains unclear. I have to wonder if Mr. Buckland
was aware of this when he broke from his Gardnerian roots
and named his new tradition Seax Wica rather than *Seax
Wicca*, as the use of one 'c' rather than two does not significantly change the meaning of the word.

As the size of the Wiccan movement grew, so did its
members' curiosity about its origins. Inevitably, the search
for answers leads back to Mr. Gardner. Sometimes called
the "Father of Modern Witchcraft," Mr. Gardner's influence was much greater than simply choosing an inappropriate name for this rebirth of Witchcraft. Many of the
practices he inspired seem to be based on either a poor
examination of history or an active libido. Ritual nudity,
called going skyclad, tops this list. There are legitimate historical accounts of ritual nudity, but Mr. Gardner empha-
sized being skyclad during his rites more than the legitimate
accounts would seem to dictate. Later supporters of Gardner
would look to medieval prints of Witches and note that a
great deal of them depicted ritual nudity. Of course they
did! The Church considered nudity sinful. Most of those
prints were created by the Church and Church followers to

slander Pagan practices. Many of these same type of prints depict the kissing of goats on the rear end, the stirring of babies into cauldrons, and the worship of the Christian concept of the antagonist Satan. They cannot be used as reliable sources for information.

Other practices that can be traced to Mr. Gardner, albeit not exclusively, include the use of the scourge (a small whip) by the High Priestess to maintain order, the initiation of men by only women, and the garter as rank insignia for the High Priestess. A typical Gardnerian initiation involved nudity, bondage, and flagellation. While each of these practices does have some historical reference, why he chose to bring them together and emphasize them can be a matter of much debate.

I am heartfully thankful for Mr. Gardner's role in making modern Witchcraft available, but I also feel that it is necessary to allow the movement to grow beyond the narrow parameters of his tradition. Today, Wiccans realize they have the diverse cultural heritage of all people as sources of inspiration.

The Future of Wicca

Today, Wicca fulfills the spiritual needs of tens of thousands of people. It is very likely that its numbers will continue to grow. The rebirth of the old ways has come at a time when their tenets are infinitely sensible. In a society where all living things are gaining value, Wicca teaches that life is sacred—not just that of human beings, but all life. Many Wiccans, myself included, are strict vegetarians. Others eat meat solemnly and often thank the spirit of the animal for its sacrifice. In the past, the rights of animals were barely considered by Western society. In modern times, we have established organizations like the American Society for the

Prevention of Cruelty to Animals. States and other regulatory organizations have enacted laws providing specific penalties for the harming of animals. While Christianity continues to teach that man has been given "dominion over the fish of the sea, and over the fowl of the air, and over every living thing" (Gen. 1:28), Wicca teaches that we must live in harmony with fish, fowl, and every living thing, that we do not have dominion over any living thing except ourselves.

The ancients knew that the earth was what sustained their existence. It is sometimes argued that environmental concerns did not grow until the Industrial Age, but that is not necessarily true. When living off the land, it is clearly necessary to be concerned about overhunting, overdraining, and soil erosion. Although the ancients may not have achieved a global concern, without a personal concern they surely would have perished.

Modern society has created the Environmental Protection Agency and similar organizations to safeguard the earth as well as her water and air. As ancient traditions are revived, the earth has once again become sacred. Although we have moved from the countryside and into the cities, relying on grocery stores rather than the land, the recent rise in earth consciousness has reminded us that the air over Detroit is the same air that will one day be over Boise.

While the majority of society supports the introduction of laws aimed at preventing hate crimes, organizations like the Ku Klux Klan wave the Christian cross as a rallying banner. The so-called Aryan Nation and other white supremacist organizations claim similar connections to Christianity. In contrast, Wicca stands wholly against racism. In fact, although Wicca originally drew heavily on the Celtic tradition, much of the pre-Christian European tribal structure was destroyed during the Great Darkness. Thus, in an effort to restructure what has been lost, Wicca now draws on

Native American, African, and Australia's aboriginal traditions. During the persecution of Witches, the Witch hunters were not restrained to torturing only the Celts. Neither were their later counterparts. Tituba, a slave in Salem, wasn't Celtic, yet she was accused of being a Witch.

As Wicca moves further from the narrow teachings of its founders, the term Wicca will grow to encompass even more concepts and ideas. As the Church that persecuted the Witches of old had a broad definition of Witchcraft, so should the Wiccans of today have a broad definition of Wicca. As our society's fascination with magick, divination, and reincarnation grows, Wicca embraces these practices and ideas as yet another facet of nature. Today's Wiccans, like the Witches of old, do not differentiate between magick, religion, and prayer. Each is seen as a part of nature. Most Wiccans perceive little difference between praying and burning a candle with intent.

Because Wicca and Neo-Paganism are suited to our modern social and ethical views, they will continue to grow. Today, Wiccans and members of similar religions can be found in every walk of life. Over the years, I have met Wiccans who are authors, lawyers, doctors, nurses, soldiers, teachers, and law enforcement officers. Recently, a Hollywood celebrity thanked the Goddess on national television after receiving an award. A daytime soap opera has featured a Wiccan character. Outspoken Wiccans with no other claim to fame have been given the spotlight by local and national news programs. I have discussed Wicca on television and radio numerous times simply because I own a Neo-Pagan store. Wiccan and Pagan celebrations, festivals, and conventions are springing up everywhere. The message that Wicca is available, applicable, and accessible is being heard. As its tenets become more widely known, its growth will become exponential.

Unfortunately, there are people who have not divorced the type of thinking that led to the destruction of the old religions. Hopefully, in time, they will realize that one person's Wicca is not necessarily the next person's Wicca. This is as it was in the past and it is the only way it will work in the future. Gay, straight, black, white, same struggle, same fight!

3

The Gods and Goddesses

It is often difficult to properly explain Wicca as a religion because our society has been dominated by a belief system alien to the teachings of nature. Our language often makes it difficult to express concepts which are at the very root of nature-based religions.

Even the word religion often denotes concepts not in harmony with the Wiccan path. When one considers the word *religion* to mean "re-legion" or "re-joining," it is easy to understand how this word might seem inappropriate. In the more mainstream belief systems, religion means rejoining with a supernatural God, a force which is removed and apart from this world. To the followers of those ways, religion is a way to remove oneself from what is natural, to ascend from the earth, and enter the heavens to rejoin their God at the point of death.

In Wicca, the idea of rejoining with God or Goddess is available in the here and now, without the wait for death. When a Wiccan makes love to a woman, he is rejoining his Goddess in the most intimate way possible, at the point of

23

life rather than death. The Wiccan understands that each
person is a part of nature and that the Lord and Lady are
incarnated as all things that are natural. The Wiccan religion
is the process that rejoins the Wiccan with the earth and all
things natural. So although the word religion applies to
Wicca, its meaning is separate from that of other religions.

The words *belief* and *faith* can often be used synony-
mously with religion when referring to the dominant Western religions. But these synonyms are only appropriate
when the religion being discussed has a basis that is distinctly separate from what can be observed by the senses.
The words faith and belief should only be used when it is
necessary to have faith to believe in deity. The Wiccan no
more *believes* in deity than one believes in a tree. The tree
is real, we can touch it, climb it, and fall from it. We
require no faith to know that it exists. It is there.

Similarly confused, the word worship is not accurate
when describing the act of honoring the Wiccan view of
deity. Our Gods and Goddesses are our parents, our lovers,
and our friends. Although they are worthy of our worship,
they do not demand it. Instead, they welcome our love and
respect, asking that we honor their incarnation, which can
be seen in every living thing.

As there was no central doctrine for the Pagans and
Witches of old, there is no central doctrine for today's
Wicca. In the past, customs, traditions, and views of God
and Goddess (often called the Lord and Lady) varied from
one person to the next. In many areas of the world, each
village had its own patron deity. Modern Wicca is much the
same. The practice changes with the community in which it
is found, varying from coven to coven, and even from Wiccan to Wiccan. While deity imagery is often taken directly
from the mythology of ancient peoples, modern forms are
just as welcome. The most local of these are personal

deities. Having a personal deity allows you to have a deep relationship with that deity. Whenever I fire my kiln, my own personal kiln God sits on top of the lid. There, he guards the kiln's contents against bad happenstance.

The union between the Wiccan and deity is a marriage. In Creation's Covenant, a ring or other symbol of devotion is donned during the self-dedication rite, much like an engagement ring. During the initiation rite into a coven, a second ring, or "wedding ring," is placed on the right hand. This marriage between Wiccan and creator is facilitated by the Wiccan view of deity. The male Wiccan views Goddess as the perfect partner (wife) in life. He views God as all things he is and aspires to be.

At different points in history, in different regions, and within different groups, these central concepts of deity have acquired individual names. In the past, the root concept of God evolved into a pantheon of Gods: Apollo, Cernunnos, Cronos, Thor, Odin, Pan, and thousands more. Similarly, Goddess evolved into Venus, Demeter, Hecate, Diana, Isis, Astarte, and a multitude equal to the Gods. But always at the root of the diversity is the simple emulation of male and female. The archetypes of old are still used. Today, most Wiccans acknowledge that these seemingly separate deities are parts of the whole, of the concept of deity.

Wiccans see Goddess in all women and God in all men, including oneself. If, after centuries of being told how sinful we are, it is difficult for you to believe that you are God incarnate, think of it in terms of the relationship between yourself and your father. As your earthly father is a clear part of the man that you are, so God is a clear part of the spiritual being that you are—but there are differences. As long as you remember that each and every living thing is also the incarnation of deity, it isn't a pompous or wholly self-serving concept.

Men and Goddess

It has been said that although men may praise Goddess,
they can not truly know her. Mystery is an attraction. It is
the spark of desire. Rather than being a hindrance to men
in their praise of Goddess, longing for what they do not
know is the passion that drives men to adore her. This drive
increases the attraction of Goddess to men and thus their
exploration. Because the Wiccan male sees his Goddess in
every woman, when he makes love to a woman, he is making love to his Goddess.

As the natural stages of human life are youth, midlife,
and twilight, Goddess is often described in the same manner and referred to as the Triple Goddess. The stages of
Goddess are the Maiden, Mother, and Crone. In relationship to her aspect as Moon Goddess, she is the waxing
(Maiden), the full (Mother), and the waning (Crone) moon.

The Maiden is is the innocent virgin, and because her
next stage is the mother, the not-so-innocent flirt. She is the
tomboy who slugged you when you were a boy. She is the
one girl you let into your tree fort, maybe the one who
helped you build the thing. She is the best friend that the
other boys made fun of you for having, the one you constantly defended from their childish rants. As you both
grew, she became the best friend the other boys praised you
for having.

She respected your chivalry, never letting you know that
she was not in need of your protection. Then, without
notice, she became the huntress. Like a cat, she often
toyed with her prey before the final strike. Because of her
playful nature, you were never sure exactly what she was
stalking. Sometimes it was knowledge and new ideas,
sometimes the answers to her insatiable curiosity, sometimes you.

The Maiden is the muse of the artist. She is the waxing and growing moon. In her later stages, she is the woman that all men desire, but also the one who is almost always just out of reach. She is the focus of Pan's antics. She is all things new and all things growing.

The later stages of the Maiden Goddess are that of the warrior and huntress, like Athena (Greek), who is said to

Sun Goddesses and Their Origins

Goddess	*Origin*
Amaterasu	Japanese
Ba'alat	Phoenician
Bast	Egyptian
Gauri	Indian
Grainne	Irish
Hae-Sun	Korean
Hathor	Egyptian
Hsi Wang Mu	Chinese
Igaehinduo	Cherokee
Sabazius	Greek
Saule	Baltic
Sakhmet	Egyptian
Sequineq	Eskimo
Shapash	Sumerian
Sulis	British
Surya	Hindu
Tsu	Yucchi
Unelanuhi	Cherokee
Ushas	Hindu
Vesta	Roman
Walu	Australian Aboriginal
Wurusemu	Hittite
Yhi	Australian Aboriginal

Moon Goddesses and Their Origins

Goddess	*Origin*
Aataentsic	Iroquois
Aine of Knockaine	Irish
Al-Lat	Persian
Anu	Celtic
Arianrhod	Welsh
Ashtaroth	Phoenician
Auchimalgen	Araucanians
Bendis	Greek
Black Annis	Celtic
Brigantis	Celtic
Brigit	Celtic
Brizo	Greek
Callisto	Greek
Caridwen	Welsh
Changing Woman	Navajo
Ch' Ang-O	Chinese
Chia	Columbian
Circe	Greco-Roman
Coatlicue	Aztec
Cybele	Celtic
Europa	Italian
Fana	Italian
Freya	Norse
Frigga	Germanic
Hainvwele	Indonesian
Hera	Greek
Hina	Tahitian
Holle	Teutonic
Hun-Ahpu-Mtye	Guatemalan
Hunthaca	Colombian
Inda	Hindu
Inanna	Sumerian
Io	Greek

Goddess	Origin
Ishtar	Babylonian
Isis	Egyptian
Ixchel	Mayan
Jana	Roman
Juno	Roman
Jyotsna	Hindu
Ka-ata-killa	Pre-Inca
Komorkis	Blackfoot
Lilith	Sumerian
Luna	Roman
Morgana	Celtic
Nuah	Babylonian
Pe	African
Persephone	Greek
Sarasvati	Indian
Sedna	Inuit
Selene	Greek
Shingo-Moo	Chinese
Sina	Polynesian
Sirdu	Chaldaean

have been born in full armor. She is the protector of thought and expression, especially in the arts. She is also Diana (Roman) and Artemis (Greek), each a huntress who communes with nature. She guards the forests and deep woods, lending her accuracy and clarity of focus when we need it.

She is the curious and sometimes mischievous Goddess Eris (Greek), whose practical jokes have led to war. She is the spirit of casting stones just to see the ripples in the water. She is the Goddess of physical love, Aphrodite (Greek). Ostara (Teutonic), whose name led to the celebration of "Easter," is also a maiden Goddess, as are numerous others. In these later stages, she becomes your perfect lover.

Call on her to improve sexual relationships, but remember that she is already present in all women.

The Maiden Goddess grows into the Mother Goddess as the waxing moon grows into the full moon. Diana grows into the mother, Aradia (Italian). In her Mother aspect, Goddess is nurturing and sharply watchful of her children. From her womb comes all life, from her breasts all sustenance. This is why she is linked so closely to the earth.

This is where perspectives get tricky. She is your nurturer and mother only when you view her through the eyes of a child. When seeing her as an adult, she nurtures you the way life partners nurture each other. This is expressed in the modern custom of sharing cake after a wedding The bride feeds the groom at the same time the groom feeds the bride. She becomes the perfect mother of your children, nurturing them as your mother nurtured you.

It is widely believed that the Mother Goddess was our first concept of the divine. She can be found in almost every culture and religion, including early Christianity. While the Father, the Son, and the Holy Spirit might currently be thought of as entirely male, the original Hebrew concept for the trinity held that the Holy Spirit was definitively female. This trinity can then be said to equate to the natural trinity of life: the father, the mother, and the children.

She is the fertility Goddesses of the earth Astarte (Canaanite) and Bona Dea (Roman), she is Earth Mother Gaia (Greek) and Demeter, (Greek) Goddess of the fruitfulness of the earth. In a time when the survival of our race depended strongly on these aspects of nature, she became so entrenched in our cultural psyche that even the last two thousand years of Christianity have not removed her. Outside the Neo-Pagan community, the concept of "Mother Earth" and "Mother Nature" is easily seen and heard. Television weather announcers still speak of her and many farmers, travelers, and fans of outdoor activities still pray to her. Until recently, tropical storms carried only female names. Mother is the teacher and administrator of parental authority on a global scale. Take the advice from folklore, personal observation, or common sense—the warning seems clear: don't fool with Mother Nature.

Contrary to the more prevalent view that divinity works in mysterious ways, the fact is that divinity and humanity have a cause-and-effect relationship. In much the same way we have burned ourselves on pots of boiling water, the Earth Mother responds to our use of chlorofluorocarbons by decreasing the ozone layer. As our earthly mother warned us about the pot of boiling water, our Earth Mother warned us about harming the environment. Whether or not we are burned is entirely up to us.

As life cycles draw close to their end, so the cycle of the moon moves from full to dark. Of the three aspects of Goddess, the Crone is probably the most misunderstood. With typical Halloween decorations including old hags with warts on their long noses, she is certainly the most slandered. The Crone is the Grandmother aspect of Goddess. Her strength rests in knowledge gathered over a lifetime. She is tempered and concise.

In the same way a mother lends assistance to her pregnant daughter, the Crone is the protector of women during childbirth. This is her Grandmother aspect. Make no mistake, the Grandmother not only retains her maternal instincts but extends these instincts in an umbrella over her grandchildren.

Viewed from the eyes of the young, the Crone is the Grandmother. Viewed from the eyes those in the midlife, she is the Mother. Viewed from the later stages, she is the partner that you committed to growing old with. As Cerridwen (Welsh), she stirs her cauldron of knowledge, offering the

wisdom to use it. As Hecate (Greek), she is the Goddess of
the crossroads and of decisions. Call to her when decision
making becomes difficult. She is the grandmother who tucks
us in when we are sick and the one who comes when we die,
preparing us to awaken with a new body.

Men and God

The atrocity of removing the Goddess from our lives pales
in comparison to the horrors of what our God has been
turned into. While many no longer recognize the Goddess
Diana, they are fairly sure who her brother Lucifer is. They
are wrong.

Although many Christians are quick to relate the horns
of a proud God of the hunt with their myths of Satan, there
is absolutely no connection other than the misconceptions
of the Church. The concept of a horned hunter God dates
well beyond the Christian invention of an all-evil horned
opponent to their God—possibly as far back as the dawn
of humanity.

The saddest part of this thinking is that it has deeply
affected not only those who believe the slanders against old
Gods, but also those who are attempting to renew the old
ways. After so many generations of misinformation, even
those who are rediscovering the old ways have difficulty
relating to the male half of divinity because they are concerned about falling into the same "God is male" trap again.

Rejecting the male half of divinity as a rebellion against
male-dominated religions is foolish. It allows those religions
to continue their control over your thoughts. Choosing how
one sees deity is a serious decision and should not be made
out of rebellion. If you have chosen Wicca as your spiritual
path, be Wiccan to be Wiccan, not to be non-Christian.

If you were raised Christian, as many Wiccans were, you have probably received the traditional warnings about God and his punishments. If we started a list of the things that the Christian God will send you to Hell for, we would run out of paper long before we ran out of sins. "Don't try to hide from him," Christian children are told, "He is everywhere and sees everything you do." After being told time and time again that God is an all-powerful bogeyman in the sky, it can be hard to embrace him as a creator of life. But the Wiccan must do just this. The Wiccan must cast off the mistruth that God is condemning and judgmental, saving the rewards of his kingdom for only a select few of his children. The male half of divinity does not play favorites. He is above all else, our loving father. With Goddess, he has given us the gift of life that we might share it with all of creation.

Like the Triple Goddess, the Horned God is seen in many cultures in the three stages of life: the Son, the Father, and the Sage. As the Sun God, he has two cycles, and three phases in each. He is the dawn, day, and dusk and he is the full solar year: waxing, full, and waning.

As the Son, he is the dawn and the time shortly after Winter Solstice. He is the child that lives forever in every man. He is Loki (Teutanic), the practical joker, always ready to pull out the chair just before you sit down. He is our inspiration in mischief. In childhood, he is our best friend, the one with which we shared our innermost boyhood secrets.

He is Cernunnos (Celtic), Pan (Greek), Faunus (Roman), and each of the Satyrs (Greek), forever chasing the nymphs through the woods, rarely catching the object of desire, but reveling in the hunt.

As he gains confidence, he becomes Eros (Greek) and Amor (Roman) who typify his attributes as lover so strongly

Sun Gods and Their Origins

God	*Origin*
Agni	Hindu
Ahura Mazda	Persian
Amun-Rae	Egyptian
Anansi	African
Anu	Babylonian
Apollo	Greek and Roman
Apu Panchau	Incan
Atum	Egyptian
Babbar	Sumerian
Baldur	Scandinavian
Bel	Babylonian
Da-Bog	Slavonic
Dagda	Celtic
Dahzhog	Slavic
Dharme	Hindu
Dumuzi	Sumerian
El	Hebrew
Freyr	Scandinavian
Helios	Greek
Hermakhis	Egyptian
Hiruku	Japanese
Horus	Egyptian
Huitzllopochtli	Aztec
Hyperion	Greek
Indra	Hindu
Inti	Inca
Janus	Roman
Khepera	Egyptian
Kinich-Ahau	Mayan
Llew Llaw Gyffes	Welsh
Lucifer	Tuscan and Judeo-Christian
Manco Capac	Incan
Mandulis	Nubian

God	Origin
Mao	Benin
Marduk	Sumerian
Maui	Polynesian
Melkart	Phoenician
Merodach	Babylonian
Mithras	Persian
Nah-Hunte	Assyro-Babylonian
Odhinn	Norse
Perun	Slavonic
Ra	Egyptian
Samas	Sumerian
Shakura	Pawnee
Shamash	Babylonian
Sin	Haidan
Sol	Roman
Svarog	Slavic
Tezctlipoca	Aztec
Tonatiuh	Aztec
Upulero	Indonesian
Varuna	Hindu
Vaseduva	Hindu
Vishnu	Hindu
Vulcan	Roman
Xiuhtecuti	Aztec

that their very names have become a part of language to describe love itself. Dionysus (Greek) and Bacchus (Roman) testify to his interest in other physical pleasures. He turns joy and pleasure into a sacrament.

He is also Ares (Greek) and Mars (Roman), and other gods of war. He is the defender of his family and of his tribe. He is the guardian of the home in times of peace but also the proud soldier gone off to defend his country and way of life.

Moon Gods and Their Origins

God	Origin
Aah	Egyptian
Alako	Romany
Alignak	Eskimo
Aningahk	Inuit
Baiame	Australian Aboriginal
Chandra	Hindu
Fati	Polynesian
Gou	Benin
Ilah	Semitic
Ilmaqah	Semitic
Itzamna	Mayan
Jacy	Brazilian
Khons	Egyptian
Mah	Persian
Mait' Carrefour	Haitian Voodoo
Mani	Nordic
Maui	Polynesian
Menu	Lithuanian
Metzli	Aztec
Myestas	Slavonic
Nanna	Sumerian
Nannar	Chaldaean
Osirius	Egyptian
Ptah	Egyptian
Sin	Sumerian
Soma	Hindu
Somas	Greek
Somantha	Hindu
Susanowo	Japanese
Tangaroa	Samoan
Taukiyomi	Japanese
Thoth	Egyptian
Toruguenket	Brazilian

God	Origin
Tsuki-yomi	Japanese
Varuna	Indu
Yarikh	Canaanite

In his Father aspect, he is the day and the Summer Solstice; the time when all things grow. He can still be found in your local garden store. There his image appears as the Green Man, a face made of leaves, defiantly smiling through the ignorance of the average customer or shop owner. He is the fertility god Apollo (Greek and Roman) and the Dagda (Irish), whose huge club has become legend. (And what of Dagda's club? In the very way the fertility of the Mother was venerated with images that had huge breasts and hips, the fertility of the father has been celebrated in references to his genitalia. Be it Dagda's club or the *long-handed* Lugh [Irish], I think the trend is fairly clear.)

Father is his Goddess's consort and life partner. He is the accomplished lover, comfortable in the knowledge that with maturity comes stamina and skill. He is the man that Wiccan men aspire to be.

He is the blacksmith, forging magickal tools in the tradition of his father, now Grandfather. He has each of the skills that you seek to possess. He is Thor (Teutonic), the protector of the working man, particularly in lower-income brackets. He is responsible for the fruits and rewards of our labor. He is the one to call on when we have problems with management at work.

He loves his children equally, but often affords a little more leeway to his sons; he is always watching and ready to pull us from harm. Where the Mother Goddess might respond differently, he greets a son's broken arm with joy as a lesson well learned.

The Sage is his elder attribute. Often our society does not seem interested in honoring the elderly, especially men. But the image of the honored elder man as the keeper of wisdom is prevalent. Who hasn't heard of Father Time? Grandfather Time would be more accurate. He is the Old King El (Semitic) and Odin (Teutonic), the keeper of infinite knowledge. Although more traditional Western views might label him as a dirty old man, the Sage with Maiden as lover is a classic image.

He is Merlin of Arthurian legend, the gifted seer of the future. He is the image of the elder Druid, making the gaining of wisdom appear so damn easy. He is the village elder, always consulted before the hunt.

The Sage is the God of Kings, the grandfather who brought you gifts that were just a bit more lavish than those your parents gave you. He rejoices in his years because it is his age which brings him to his great stature.

The Lord and Lady United
as Our Parents

Above all else, the Lord and Lady are our parents and the parents that we seek to be. When united, they are the creators of all life. Together, they are all life. Like our earthly parents, they have given us the gift of existence. They have provided sustenance and shelter. They have given us the free will to make our own decisions and mistakes, but they have always watched over us.

Creation's Covenant expresses the union of Lord and Lady, with all things that have come from their union, as the Holy Trinity of the father, the mother, and the children. There is a common hand gesture to express this trinity. First place one open hand on the other, palms up. Touch the left shoulder with both hands facing inward to honor the Mother, then move to the right shoulder to honor the Father. Next, touch the womb or genitalia to honor the potential for children. Move hands upward from the womb or genitalia, with palms facing the body, to the forehead. Then, move the hands down with palms up, in a gesture of offering. This is a sacred greeting and parting in Creation's Covenant. When it is offered to you, it indicates that although you are a child of your mother (Goddess) and your father (God), you have the freedom to choose your own view. Love can only be given; it cannot be taken. To indicate that you understand and that you agree, the movements are reversed. Place both hands on the forehead. This affirms that you have made the decision to accept the fact that you are the child (move your hands to your womb or genitalia) of the Lady (move your hands to your left shoulder) and Lord (move your hands to your right shoulder). This greeting is known as the Wiccan cross. It has also become a way of asking if a person is a member of Creation's Covenant.

As we have matured, many of us have moved far from our earthly parents. In our homes away from home, we keep reminders of where we came from: perhaps a picture of Dad or the quilt that Mom made for us when we went off to college. As humanity has matured, we have moved far away from our Earth Mother and Father. Still, we keep reminders: a garden on the patio and a furry critter on the bed. We do not need to move back in with our parents to have them in our lives, and in the same respect, we don't need to forsake civilization and move into a cave or the forest to live with our Gods and Goddesses.

The Future of the Gods

In Wiccan view, deity has been a living, growing, and changing thing. From the first concept of the fertility goddess to the incredible diversity of cultural Gods and Goddesses, our perception has changed as we have changed. This relationship between deity and humanity continued right up until the time their praise was all but stifled by the stagnant Darkness, but has picked up once again.

Because the old Gods and Goddesses had been repressed for a time, they hadn't the opportunity to grow as we have grown. To correct this, we must make a conscious effort to include them in our modern lives. We must retain our connections to the earth and allow deity into many of the things we have not traditionally thought of as natural settings for religion.

During childbirth, prayers to the Crone are just as effective from the birthing room of a major hospital as they are from deep within an elder forest. In what we create, if we consider the fact that we are creatures of nature, the lines between what we consider natural and unnatural become less defined. Yes, the hospital has a sterile and antiseptic smell, but the setting was created by natural beings for the purpose of assuring the safe birth of our children. What structure could be more holy?

In times of war, it is still more than appropriate to call upon the Gods of war to give a loved one the strength and courage necessary to return safely from military service. In times of peace, the Warrior aspects of divinity can be called upon to help in other matters. It would not be unheard of for a Wiccan to invite Thor to help forge the magickal tool to solve a conflict, even if that tool takes the form of paperwork which resolves an audit. Now that the Internet is quickly replacing the printed word, we must invite deity into cyberspace. Who better than the Crone and Sage to watch over the Information Superhighway?

In these and so many other ways, the Gods and Goddesses of old can become personal driving forces in our modern lives. They can give us the strength, wisdom, and courage to meet the daily challenges in the office, the home, and the community. However, only if we allow them into the whole of our lives can they become even a part of our lives.

4

Magick, Spellcraft, Superstition, and Magickal Ethics

The single most frequently asked question about Witchcraft is: "Does it really work?" My response is to explain that Witchcraft is a religion. Does any religion work? Of course it does. Each religion fulfills the spiritual needs of those who are content to follow its path, otherwise the religion would become extinct. Before the Dark Ages, there was little separation between magick and religion. There was also little separation between magick and science. Then the Church effectively divided the world into two camps: God and all that the Church approved of; and Satan and all that they didn't approve of. Magick and science were tossed in with Satan.

Magick

Although some consider magick nonsense, most believe that it can't hurt. Few still subscribe to the rumor that the Church state spread about magick being demonic. Belief in magick has been present from almost the very beginning of humanity's existence. It has been the tool of prince and pauper, rich and poor.

Today magick is practiced openly. Prayer, faith healing, and the lighting of candles in the hopes of causing change are all acts of magick. Tarot readers have become almost commonplace in urban markets. Astrological guides to love and romance are found in the checkout aisles of many supermarkets as well as in most newspapers and libraries. Lucky rabbit's feet are sold outside bingo halls. Who hasn't seen a psychic hotline infomercial recently?

Magick, spelled with a k to distinguish it from magic, which is sleight of hand, has been defined a thousand ways by as many people. We'll call this number one thousand and one:

Magick is science that has not been explained. The inverse of this definition is also applicable: "*Science is magick that has been explained.*"

Unfortunately, the moment magick is defined, it is no longer magick, it is science. Nevertheless, most people either knowingly or unknowingly use magick on a daily basis. Consider the job interview where the candidate enters with relaxed confidence, believing ahead of time that he will receive the position. He has dressed in a manner in which he believes others in the office may be dressed, perhaps slightly nicer. Even without knowledge of what he is doing, the candidate is observing two of the oldest patterns of magick:

Like attracts like. By dressing and conducting himself accordingly, he has made himself "like" the work environment.

Internal visualizations tend to manifest in external tangibles. To present himself as relaxed and confident, the candidate has created within himself the mind-set of belonging to the company he wishes to join. He has visualized already working there.

Recognizing these patterns is what helped bring a former lover into my life. Knowing that she has a degree in zoology and absolute commitment to saving what humanity has not yet destroyed, I had a good starting point. I knew that she had an affection for frogs, an affection so deep that she is known as the Frog Lady. Drawing on my experience as a sculptor, I created her form in clay while I visualized her taking form in my life. When I was finished, I saw that I had sculpted a young lady standing atop a frog in the same pose the Goddess Isis is often sculpted atop a scarab. Not only was I asking that she enter my life, but that she become my Goddess. After firing the piece, I kept it with me at all times. Soon, I didn't need the statue because I had the real thing.

The downside to using a magick spell is it works whether or not we want it to. Even when we are fully aware of magickal influence, once the wheels are rolling, it is often hard to bring magick to a halt. This seems to reflect natural law:

Magick in motion tends to stay in motion. Magick is not a faucet that we can turn on or off, it is a river that never runs dry. We can redirect its flow and we can even swim against its current, but we cannot eliminate its effects. If you do not respect its currents, you can easily drown. When you are in a rut, you are likely to attract the very attributes that placed you in the rut. If you walk into a job interview or ask a potential lover on a date while thinking you will be rejected, you will probably get exactly what you expect. This will continue until you either break the cycle or find yourself so convinced of failure that you simply no longer try. The other downside is that magick works. Frivolous use

is often painful. After using magick to help bring the Frog
Lady into my life, the relationship failed dismally.

It is not necessary to fully understand an event to make
use of your knowledge of the event. Once we recognize a
pattern, we can predict with reasonable certainty the out-
come of an event or sequence of actions. At one point, it
was believed that our sun revolved around the earth. Even
with this incorrect assumption, the sunrise and sunset could
easily be predicted and relied upon. It was a recognized,
though not fully understood, pattern.

Effect can be traced to cause. Two seemingly unrelated
events can be connected by recognizing cause and effect.
Consider early man before he connected sex with pregnancy. Sex seemed to have no more link to conception than
eating certain foods. Then it was observed that only women
who were sexually active would become pregnant. Once
the relationship was observed, it became clear that sex was the
cause of pregnancy.

Cause cannot always be traced to effect. Although
effect (as in pregnancy) can be traced to cause (the union
of sperm and egg), the inverse is not always true and can
cause you to make a wrong assumption. We cannot take
the cause (the union of sperm and egg) and assure an
effect (pregnancy).

Sometimes a spell just doesn't take the first time. Even
when you think you have reproduced a pattern that has
worked before, it is impossible to duplicate every possible
variable. It helps to experiment and keep a journal.
Record as many details as possible: time of day, day of
week, moon phase, mood, dress, and anything else that
might help establish the pattern to a successful magickal
practice. If you are serious about magick, you will benefit

greatly from a course in basic logic, given at almost any university.

Spellcraft and Why It Works

The term spellcraft can be used to describe the magick of both the modern and the ancient Witch. It is what Dr. Margaret Murray referred to as "operational witchcraft." While the term magick can apply to any occurrence that is not easily explained—premonition, divination, psychic abilities, aromatherapy, mind over matter, herbal medicine—spellcraft specifically denotes the making or crafting of a spell. Often it involves the use of props such as candles, incense, and oils.

Props in spellcraft are used to help the practitioner focus both conscious and subconscious thought. A black human-shaped candle might be used during a healing ritual. As the black wax melts away, one visualizes the illness burning away. This simple spell works also with a green candle, the favored color of healing. With a green candle, the visualization is that the candle is the person to be healed and the flame is a white healing energy burning into the body.

In many binding spells, cords are tied around dolls. Few serious practitioners believe the cord being tied around the doll has a magick energy of its own. The act of wrapping the doll and visualizing the intended recipient's energy being bound is simply a focal point for the visualization.

When you consider the many ways we can impact our consciousness, you'll begin to see how spellcraft might actually work. There are a few possible explanations of how the props and other factors in spellcraft can modify our consciousness, but until their effectiveness is fully explained, these workings will remain in the realms of magick.

Color is a factor that impacts our minds through our sense of sight—age-old knowledge closely guarded by retailers. The food-service industry has figured out what colors stimulate appetite while designers of shopping malls have determined what colors encourage spending. Even the government has hopped on the color bandwagon. After studies were conducted to determine the impact of colors on violent prisoners, the holding cells of many jails were repainted. In spellcraft, color choices are made for candles, altar coverings, sachets, and other spell-related items, which set the tone for the particular spell.

Essential oils impact our minds through our sense of smell. They are a wonderful example of magick in the throes of becoming science. The essences of plants are often used in spellcraft. Patchouly, sometimes spelled patchouli, is said to attract women, while vanilla is supposed to attract men. Now that science has explored this realm, we can say with reasonable certainty that scent affects human consciousness. Not long ago, a study revealed that the scent of lavender is more effective at promoting sleep than most over-the-counter remedies. But the Witch knew this habit of information long before modern science figured it out. When you consider the great impact our mood can have on our ability to be prosperous, is it any wonder that specific scents are said to aid in prosperity?

Food and drink impact our minds through our sense of smell, taste, temperature, and direct chemical effects on both body and mind.

Herbs also impact our minds through our sense of smell and when consumed, they have direct chemical effects. In days of old, herbs were named for their appearance. Crane's bill was dove's foot and May apple was duck's foot. Many of these names have survived in modern usage, but some of the old names for herbs have created misunderstandings about Witchcraft. Hare's foot was once the common name for clover, and, of course, a four-leaf clover is supposed to bring you luck—a much less repulsive notion than finding good luck in a dead rabbit's foot.

Herbcraft is another good example of magick beginning to become science. Many herbs are powerful medicines. Some are said to inspire the act of love, others aid sleep and dreaming when placed inside a pillow. The herbs need not always be ingested to achieve a magickal or medicinal effect: When worn in sachets or burnt as incense, their scent has an impact on the human psyche.

Light conditions impact our mind through our sense of sight. Light stimulates waking states in the mind, while the lack of light stimulates nonwaking states of mind.

Weather conditions impact our minds through the sense of touch and temperature. They also affect us through chemical means. Our bodies experience specific changes when exposed to cold, warmth, darkness, and light, and anything that affects the body also affects the mind.

Seasonal changes affect our psyche in many ways—some have yet to be understood. Mental health practitioners track the effects of seasonal changes to help the recovery of clients afflicted with various mood disorders.

Repetition affects us by establishing neural pathways in which information is processed. By repeating words or activities, we create connections within our brains. Rhyme is a cousin to repetition. It is often easier to remember something that is spoken in rhyme than it is to remember the same information when it is simply spoken. Rhymes tend to continue to wander around in our minds even when we have stopped deliberately thinking of them.

Rhythm is also related to repetition. It is often possible to use drums or other rhythm-generating devices to achieve other states of consciousness. The rhythm of our bodies

moving in dance accompanied by an ever quickening drum-
beat can bring even the most relaxed person into a state of
ecstasy. A different rhythm can be wholly relaxing.

Stones, crystals, and other seemingly inanimate and non-
interactive objects are often used with great success.
Although I am not absolutely sure how they work, you'd
have a hard time convincing me that the malachite in each
corner of my store is a bad idea. There is strong evidence
that vibration factors are at work. The working theory is
that all matter vibrates at very specific rates. Bloodstone,
which is said to have healing properties, may vibrate at a
frequency conducive to healing, while rose quartz, believed
widely to attract love, may vibrate at a frequency which
encourages us to be receptive to love.

A system of planetary cycles for spellcraft was devised
thousands of years ago. Although I have found these cycles
less important than other factors in spellcraft, if they are
convenient to use, they cannot hurt. When these systems
were developed, the sun, moon, and five other heavenly
bodies were called planets. Magickal associations were
made with each planet. Later each planet and its attributes
was associated with a specific day of the week.

The night was also seen as having planetary associations.
At night, the associations are connected to periods of planetary dominance. Each night has twelve periods. I have used
the term "periods" to refer to the time that each planet
rules. Often these times are called "planetary hours."
Because the time between the start and end of a planetary
rulership is sixty minutes only on an equinox, I feel the
term "hour" is misleading. I have also used letters instead
of numbers for extra clarity.

You are likely to find reference to the first or second
period of a planet. Some planets have two periods of time
which they rule in a single night. The first period of planetary

Planetary Associations and the Days of the Week

Day of Week	Planetary Association	Magickal Associations and Attributes
Sunday	Sun	Employment, leadership, healing, male divinity
Monday	Moon	Growth, family, medicine, dreams, female divinity
Tuesday	Mars	War, competition, conflict, lust, courage, hunting
Wednesday	Mercury	Education, divination, intelligence, communication
Thursday	Jupiter	Money, luck, gambling, tangible prosperity, law
Friday	Venus	Love, partnership, union, pleasure, art, music
Saturday	Saturn	Endings, divorce, funerals, death, reincarnation

Planetary Associations of the Night

Period	Sun.	Mon.	Tues.	Wed.	Thur.	Fri.	Sat.
A	Jupiter	Venus	Saturn	Sun	Moon	Mars	Mercury
B	Mars	Mercury	Jupiter	Venus	Saturn	Sun	Moon
C	Sun	Moon	Mars	Mercury	Jupiter	Venus	Saturn
D	Venus	Saturn	Sun	Moon	Mars	Mercury	Jupiter
E	Mercury	Jupiter	Venus	Saturn	Sun	Moon	Mars
F	Moon	Mars	Mercury	Jupiter	Venus	Saturn	Sun
G	Saturn	Sun	Moon	Mars	Mercury	Jupiter	Venus
H	Jupiter	Venus	Saturn	Sun	Moon	Mars	Mercury
I	Mars	Mercury	Jupiter	Venus	Saturn	Sun	Moon
J	Sun	Moon	Mars	Mercury	Jupiter	Venus	Saturn
K	Venus	Saturn	Sun	Moon	Mars	Mercury	Jupiter
L	Mercury	Jupiter	Venus	Saturn	Sun	Moon	Mars

Planetary Hours

Period	Begins	Ends
A	5:17 P.M.	6:30 P.M.
B	6:30 P.M.	7:43 P.M.
C	7:43 P.M.	8:56 P.M.
D	8:56 P.M.	10:09 P.M.
E	10:09 P.M.	11:22 P.M.
F	11:22 P.M.	12:35 A.M.
G	12:35 A.M.	1:48 A.M.
H	1:48 A.M.	3:01 A.M.
I	3:01 A.M.	4:14 A.M.
J	4:14 A.M.	5:27 A.M.
K	5:27 A.M.	6:40 A.M.
L	6:40 A.M.	7:53 A.M.*

*Note that even when I rounded, I was only off by one minute.

rulership is the first period to occur that night. Likewise for the second. For example, on Friday, the first period of Venus is period C and the second period of Venus is period J. On Sunday, the first period of Jupiter is A and the second period of Jupiter is H.

To find the exact beginning and ending time of these periods, it is necessary to count the minutes between sunrise and sunset and divide that number by twelve. The result is the length of each "period." Except on the equinox, this figure will never be exactly sixty minutes. The first period starts at sunset. The second begins the moment the first ends. The exact time of these events can be found in the weather section of most local newspapers. It is best to rely on local information as the times change with location. Keep in mind that the old ways teach that the day starts at sunset, not sunrise.

On the night of January 1, 2001 C.E., the sun will set at 5:17 in Columbus, Ohio. The next morning, it will rise at 7:54 AM. There are a total of 877 minutes that night. Divided by twelve you get 73.0833. Feel free to figure out the seconds, but I stick to rounding them off to seventy-three minutes per period. So on that night the following periods apply (see chart on previous page).

Superstition and the Recognition of Patterns

Superstition is also difficult to define, but I'll try: Superstition is the recognition of patterns without full understanding of why the patterns emerge. After waking to a red sky one morning, the captain of a sailing vessel informs the crew that their fishing trip would be postponed until the next morning. A second captain laughs at him, criticizing him of being superstitious, readies his ship, and sets sail.

"Red sky at night, sailors delight. Red sky at morning, sailors take warning" (an old sailor's superstition). Neither captain had the advantage of today's atmospheric science, but one chose to heed the superstition that when the sky is red in the morning, the sea will not be hospitable for sailing. Modern science can now explain that a red sunrise indicates storm conditions. While one captain was accused of being superstitious, the other never returned to port.

Few people understand exactly why the winter is cold and the summer is hot, but most recognize the pattern and dress accordingly. Although it is often considered an insult to call someone superstitious, cultural superstitions permeate our society. Some restaurants provide mints after a meal because it freshens the breath, but mint is known to many as a cure for an upset stomach. Sage is also good for settling the stomach and is found in most kitchens; it is also included in many heavy wintertime meals. I have even heard that it helps stave off winter colds, yet the average cook uses sage simply because it is called for in a recipe.

Magickal Ethics

Ethics in magick is a concept that seems to occupy an undue amount of time and consideration. It does not have to be that way. Considering the correctness of a magickal action is no different than considering the correctness of a physical action.

Magickal Ethics:	Is it acceptable to use magick to have sex with another person against that person's will?
Physical Ethics:	Is it acceptable to use force to have sex with another person against that person's will?
Magickal Ethics:	Is it acceptable to use magick to make yourself particularly attractive to a specific person?
Physical Ethics:	Is it acceptable to dress and groom to attract a specific person to you?

It is often professed by Wiccans that the Wiccan Rede specifically forbids the harming of others: "An you harm none, do what thou will." I'll stress this again because it is imperative that it is understood. Nowhere in this portion of the Rede is the Wiccan forbidden from doing harm. There are times when harm is necessary in order to protect yourself or something or someone you hold dear. Just as there are physical conditions where it is necessary to cause harm to others, there are situations where it is acceptable to use magick to cause harm. Indeed, in some situations, the Wiccan is almost duty-bound to use magick to cause harm to others.

Consider a situation where an ecologically unfriendly corporation seeks an E.P.A. variance to turn an old-growth forest into a parking lot. If magick is employed to prevent the corporation from successfully obtaining a variance, the corporation and its stockholders will suffer a monetary loss.

Magickal Ethics:	Is it acceptable to use magick to heighten awareness and sway public opinion against the corporate plans for the old-growth forest?
Physical Ethics:	Is it acceptable to use a petition or advertisement to raise public awareness in the hopes that pressure will be placed on the corporation and the E.P.A. to reconsider?
Magickal Ethics:	Is it acceptable to use magick to cause physical harm to those who infringe on the forest?
Physical Ethics:	Is it acceptable to place spikes in the trees to cause harm and death to chainsaw operators?

Acts of magick have no greater or lesser ethical consequences than more tangible physical acts. Remember that like attracts like. In the physical act of driving spikes into trees, or in the magickal act of causing harm to those who would do harm to the forest, one invites similar acts: "Unless in self defense it be, always mind the rule of three" (from the Wiccan Rede).

The rule of three, or the threefold law, dictates that everything you cast off will return to you threefold, whether it be three times good or three times bad. This return of forces cast is often called *karma*, but it is not the same thing. The concept of karma comes from the Eastern belief in a force that we tend to generate through specific and numerous actions, in various incarnations, which bind us to this realm and keep us from ascending to the next. More often than not, Wiccans believe that only negative or destructive behavior creates karma and that it is this energy that hangs around in the universe, building intensity. Then, at the absolute worst time, it slams back full force giving you at least three times the harm that you sent out.

I don't like this explanation at all. First, it seems to absolutely violate the laws of diminished return. It also seems to imply that there is a great accountant in the sky who is keeping track of every detail of our lives, multiplying our destructive nature and returning it three-fold when we can least withstand the assault. This sounds so similar to the Christian concept of Judgment Day that I am forced to believe it is perpetuated by those who have attached breasts to the Christian concept of God and titled themselves Pagan. Because of all its misconceptions, I prefer to avoid using the word karma. Instead, I recognize the rule of three and its patterns within two of the common guidelines of magick:

- *"Like attracts like"* Because thieves tend to make friends with thieves, they will have things stolen from them. Because those who choose violence as the primary method of problem solving tend to associate themselves with those of like minds, violence will likely be used against them in an effort to solve a problem.

- *"Cause and effect"* If you place your hand in fire it will burn. If you leave your hand in fire, it will continue to burn. Similarly, because there is not enough food in a country to feed its people, the people starve.

A friend who saw this manuscript before the final draft assured me that, if I express my belief in the cause-and-effect nature of karma, that I will be crucified by liberals for blaming victims. I am not blaming victims. Consider this: I said that if there is not enough food in a country to feed its people, the people will starve. Answer the following question and you will know who I blame: Who allowed there not to be enough food in the country?"

If we explain the threefold law as cause and effect, we are not placing blame, we are empowering the victim by pointing out that the cycle can be ended. Sometimes, what we have received are the effects of a bad decision (cause).

Another example is, tarot readers are often asked about the fidelity or lack of fidelity in relationships. Oftentimes, the tarot reader isn't needed to answer such questions. Are you cheating on your lover? If you answer yes, then your lover is probably cheating on you. Hence, like attracts like. If you want to be in a monogamous relationship, being monogamous will help greatly—we are directly responsible for our actions.

By understanding these principles, we can sculpt our lives and the circumstances within them. We can use magick, spellcraft, and superstition to improve our lives and our community, but only if we do so with clear intent. Without intent, as with the failed job interview, magick is used both to our own detriment and to the detriment of our community.

5

Ritual Tools

The idea of the sacred play is central to most religions. Oftentimes, these sacred plays denote pivotally important stories. Catholic mass is conducted in a scripted manner. A wafer or piece of bread and wine are shared to recreate the last supper of their sacrificial God (Christ). Jewish custom dictates the format of the seder to commemorate the freeing of the Jewish people from the slavery of Egypt. These sacred plays usually employ props or symbols. The Catholic mass utilizes an incense burner, candles, a crucifix, host holders, and a chalice. The Jewish seder uses specific food, plates, clothing, an extra place setting, and a doorway. Without these props, the symbolism of the sacred play would be missing from these religious practices. Wicca is no different.

In Wicca, the sacred plays denote the creation and natural cycles of life. These sacred plays are most frequently called rituals. The props used are known as ritual tools. Ideally, each tool should be made entirely by the practitioner who will be using it. When this is not practical, purchasing tools and customizing them in some way is acceptable. Wood can be easily carved and metal can be etched. If you encounter a tool that feels absolutely right just the way it is, you should use it just as it is. As with all things in the Craft, if it feels wrong, it is wrong.

Primary Tools

The two most important Wiccan ritual tools are the athame (a double-edged knife) and the chalice. These are the main symbols of the Lord and Lady and are used in almost every Wiccan tradition. Along with the censer (a device for burning incense) and pentacle (a round disk that represents the earth), these constitute the primary ritual tools of Creation's Covenant and are necessary for most rites. Each tool is associated with both a gender and one of the first four elements: Air, Fire, Water, and Earth. As each of these four elements is associated with one of the four directions, or quarters, so is each of the primary tools. Air is east, Fire is south, Water is west, and Earth is north. Each tool also has a complement or mate of the opposite gender. In Wiccan ritual, each tool is united with its complement or mate in a symbolic Great Rite which is a commemoration of life. By celebrating the union of male and female, Wiccans affirm that life is good.

The athame is is a ritual knife whose gender is male and whose female complement is the chalice. Although the athame has been associated with the element Air, I prefer to equate it with fire because it is a tool of rapid transformation. Although wind (air) has transformed landscapes, it does not cause change as rapidly nor with as much force as fire. The athame is thus, in my view, associated with the south quarter.

In Wiccan ritual, the athame is the primary working symbol of the Wiccan God and of all forces that are male.

It is also the single most misunderstood tool of the Craft. As all tools have the potential for misuse, the athame has been falsely depicted in movies as being used in blood sacrifice. In Wicca, the athame is never used for any physical cutting—it is honored because it represents one of the key developments of our species. In primitive fashion, it was the first tool to bring humanity out of the Stone Age. It is likely that after acquiring fire, early man found deposits of iron pooling under the stones of a fire circle, which, once cooled, made wonderful cutting and scraping tools. In time, they would deliberately select rocks rich in iron. Later, they would shape sand and dirt around the fire so that the iron puddles would take form. The use of fire to create the athame further substantiates its association with Fire.

The athame typically has a double edge, signifying the union of the God and Goddess, joined at the tip but separate along the edges. It serves to remind us that at early stages in the womb we are all female, but as we move from that point, the differences between male and female become more pronounced. A dark handle is the norm, as many believe a dark handle better absorbs energy. The athame is used to direct energy and is a tool of magickal transformation, most often being used to cast a circle. In so doing, the athame cuts through the fabric that defines this world and creates the sacred space.

In ritual, the athame represents the phallus of the Wiccan God. As the Priest represents the male half of deity, it is obvious how the athame is an incredibly personal tool for men, and how, ideally, every phase of its construction should be performed by its owner. Because this is often not possible, purchasing a custom knife or modifying a production knife is more than acceptable. If the hilt is wood, carve it with symbols that seem right for you. Many production knives can be disassembled and their handles can be replaced with one of your own design. At the very least, the athame should be personalized. If you do not have access to the tools necessary to carve or replace the hilt, you can stain, paint, or burn the hilt to fit your personality. Steel blades can be etched by carefully using a solution of two parts hydrochloric acid and one part water though a safer method is to use a chemical etching pen which may be available at your local hardware store. If these methods seem too difficult, draw the etchings on a piece of paper and bring both the drawing and the athame to a reputable gunsmith. (Attempting to get a jeweler to do this type of work is difficult as most jewelers do not have experience etching nonprecious metals.)

Many traditions have unique specifications for the athame. Some teach that its length should correspond to the length of the hand. Others insist that the athame be the length of the forearm and hand from elbow to fingertip. Choose what feels right for you. A former lover told me that she uses a pallet knife and because she is a painter, it seems to fit beautifully. Some Witches have chosen kitchen knives that have been in their family for years. Whatever your choice, make it applicable to you.

The chalice is a ritual vessel whose gender is female and whose male complement is the athame. It is associated with the element of Water and the west quarter. The chalice is to the cauldron as the athame is to the sword.

In ritual, the chalice is the primary working symbol of the Wiccan Goddess and of all forces that are female. It represents the womb of the Wiccan Goddess and is honored as the point of conception and birth. It is also a nurturing tool. It is the cupped hand of the maiden aspect of Diana lifting water to the lips of her partner in the hunt, the breast of the mother aspect of Isis as she nourishes her son Horus, and the cauldron of crone aspect of Cerridwen, whose cauldron forever nourishes her children and grandchildren.

The chalice should be either made by the practitioner or selected and personalized as carefully as the athame. Sometimes the personalizing of a chalice means nothing more than finding the finished piece that feels absolutely right. Other times, the chalice may be made of clay that was hand-dug by its owner. If you have access to a pottery kiln and want to dig your own clay, experiment with the clay before making the final piece. Different clay fuses at different temperatures. If you don't determine what you are working with, your piece could melt in the kiln or degrade into mud when you add liquid to it.

If you choose to make your own earthen chalice but do not have your own kiln, consider purchasing clay that is compatible with kilns in local ceramic shops. Most of these shops will fire your work if they are sure the firing temperatures are compatible with theirs. Ask the shop what their firing range is before buying your clay. In the ceramic trade, firing ranges are measured by a system called cones. This is a measurement of temperature and time. The cone itself is a small piece of ceramic which will bend after a specific amount of time at a specific temperature. Most ceramic shops fire at cone 04 or 05. (Remember the "0" in the cone descriptions. Cone 4 and 5 are much higher temperatures.) You'll have to let the piece dry for at least a week, have it fired, then apply food-safe glaze to at least the inside of the chalice. You can buy the glaze at the same shop. Follow the directions! Many food safe glazes are only safe when the directions are followed exactly. Avoid using crackling glaze on the inside of the chalice. Although many claim to be food safe, they may breed bacteria because it is often difficult to clean in between the tiny cracks.

After the chalice is glazed, it must be refired. To prevent cracking, it is a good idea to have the second firing at one cone lower in temperature than the first firing. This process does take more work than just buying a chalice, but the rewards of making your own tools far outweigh the inconvenience. If this seems too complicated, don't worry at all. If you ask nicely, most ceramic shopkeepers will walk you through each step as long as you are purchasing their products.

If a glass chalice is chosen, avoid leaded crystal as lead is baneful. Likewise, if you choose pewter, use only the lead-free variety. Aluminum does not react well with the acids in wine and may be harmful to the body, so avoid aluminum and aluminum-bearing metals. Silver is an excellent choice as it is associated strongly with Goddess. The downside to silver is that it oxidizes quickly, as does brass. Stoneware, porcelain, and ceramic chalices seem the optimum choice but have been known to contain lead when coming from overseas. Purchase pottery only from reputable potters. If in doubt, lead-test strips are very low in cost and are available at almost all ceramic shops.

Glass can be etched using chemicals and etching pens available at your local craft or hardware store. Metal chalices can be engraved using a special engraving tool. Do not use the electric tools that are commonly sold in department stores—these devices are fine for scratching identifying marks into home appliances, but leave jagged, unappealing lines. Most metal chalices can also be etched with acids, but different acids are used for different metals. Guides are available at most libraries. As in the case of personalizing the athame, be extremely careful when working with strong chemicals and acids.

Colorful modifications can be made to most glass and ceramic chalices with specialty products available at most craft stores. Many such stores offer a colorful variety of brush-on products which become food safe and semipermanent after being baked in a conventional oven. You will have to experiment with these, since different glass and ceramic material responds differently to the heat necessary to set the paint.

The censer is an incense burner whose gender is male and whose complement is the pentacle. The censer is associated with the element of Air and the east quarter. Smoke rising from the censer symbolizes our thoughts, prayers, and love traveling to God and Goddess, although not, as some say, because it rises to the heavens. Instead, the smoke leaves the censer as our prayers leave our circle, to touch everyone it comes in contact with before eventually joining with the cosmos.

The censer is most often metal, earthenware, or stoneware. It can be a fancy lidded device or a simple bowl with gravel at the bottom. The gravel helps air reach the incense and inhibits heat transfer to the table it rests on. If you decide to make your own censer from earthenware, you can proceed using the information presented for the chalice—but do *not* glaze the censer. Glazed censers have a tendency to crack, sometimes with tremendous force. This may happen because heat cannot be equally distributed throughout the censer. The temperature differences force areas of the censer to expand and contract differently.

The pentacle is a ritual disk whose gender is female and whose male complement is the censer. It is associated with the element of Earth and the north quarter. The pentacle is often described as a flat disk of copper, wood, or earth. I prefer an earthen disk. If you do not have access to pottery clay and a kiln, sun-dried mud or air-dry clay can also be used. For reasons which will later become clear, do not use oven-bake clay or modeling compounds that contain plastic or polymers. Likewise, it is also not a good idea to use a metal or wood pentacle for the rituals in this book.

The most common symbol to scribe upon the face of the pentacle is the pentagram (a five-pointed star within a circle). I believe this is the most appropriate symbol. The pentagram has many meanings. When displayed with one point up, its points are said to symbolize the four physical elements with the fifth element (spirit) at top. It has been used by the Pennsylvania Dutch as a protection symbol. Inverted, it is the symbol of the Horned God of Wicca and of the second degree in some traditions. In addition to these, the pentagram is the symbol of humanity, Man as Microcosm. The pentagram inscribed on the pentacle can then be considered the symbol of humanity on the earth.

The specific size of the pentacle is not important, except that it should be larger in diameter than the bottom of the censer. I use one of the ones my guild produces. It is about six inches across and about three-quarters of an inch thick with a very reflective black-and-white, marblelike glaze.

Secondary Tools

The broom is often used in Creation's Covenant Rites. Many associate the broom, often called besom, with the element Water because the broom is seen as a tool of spiritual cleansing. I prefer to associate the broom with the element Air due to the way it is used and because the broom is an obviously male tool. Associating it with the female element Water doesn't seem to fit a tool with such obvious phallic symbolism.

Historic precedent for the association can be found in numerous references to female Witches "riding brooms." This phrase was probably referring to fertility rites that were conducted exclusively by women that involved the use of symbolic but functional phallic symbols, like the broom or pole. The women would be seen riding brooms around fields and leaping into the air to show the crops how high to grow. The enjoyment of this activity was also heightened by the use of Witches' balm (flying ointment), which was applied to the broom, pole, or other functional phallic symbol. The herbal intoxicants in the balm were absorbed by the mucous membranes of the women's genitalia, causing powerful hallucinations. A word of warning: many of the herbs used to make such ointments are poisonous.

In Creation's Covenant, the broom is always decorated with bells, which serve two purposes. Bells have traditionally been used to scare away negative energy and seem to have a natural connection with the purpose of the broom, that is, cleansing. Moreover, Creation's Covenant uses the broom as a gate. The bells signal that the gate is being opened.

With visualization, the broom sweeps away a circle of negative energy before the true circle is cast. It is also used during rites of passage, placed across a door or gateway. The tradition of crossing the broom during marriage has become synonymous with the union as in the custom of "jumping the broom."

The cauldron carries the same associations as the chalice, except that due to the size difference, its complement is the sword (see page 66). The cauldron has become so associated with Witchcraft that plastic imitations are commonly sold in costume shops along with the stereotypical "Witch" costumes.

The cauldron's strong connection with Witchcraft was forged during the Burning Times and tempered in bad movies and current stereotypes. Originally the cauldron was nothing more than a cooking tool. When the country dwellers (pagans) would meet, they would often share a communal meal. As the Sabbats and Esbats are times of celebration, the fire was stoked and the cauldron filled with a feast. If by chance the pagans were discovered, they would take what they could and flee into the woods to avoid detention, torture, and death. Grabbing a one-hundred-pound hot iron cauldron from the fire was not high on the list of things to do before escaping into the night, so persecutors were often left with nothing but dinner and the cauldron it was simmered in.

Today the cauldron is most often used for ornamental reasons. Although I do not like the practice, sometimes a small cauldron is used as a censer. I feel this confuses the elemental associations, as does the practice of using large cauldrons to contain a fire. Sometimes cauldrons are filled with water and used for gazing meditations (scrying). This is often the cast at Samhain (see page 101). Personally, I would like to see a time when the cauldron is once again used for communal meals.

The gates and gate stones are ritual tools whose gender is female and whose complement is the broom. They are associated with the element Earth and the north quarter. The gate need not be physical—it can be visualized when and where it's needed. This is done by tracing a portal in the magick circle with the athame, while visualizing the gateway opening from the outer world into the sanctity of the ritual space.

The gate is the entryway to the circle and the doorway created to leave a circle once cast, but before opened. It is also used in rites of passage and in the ritual marking of a point where one life is left for another, as in the rites of adulthood or marriage. In the rite of marriage, its complement, the broom, is often laid across the gate so that the couple must cross the union of male and female, gate and broom, to be born together into their new life.

Because there is no mandate for a tangible gate, I have seen many Wiccans use this tool without realizing it. In initiation rites of some groups, newcomers enter the circle by crawling through the legs of female members. This serves to remind the initiate that it was through woman that they were born into this world. In other circles, the Priest joins his right hand with the Priestess's left hand, then with his right foot against her left, they make a diamond entrance to the circle for members to enter, serving as a reminder that it is through the union of both male and female that we entered this world.

I prefer to use gate stones. These are two flat stones which are placed three or four feet apart. They can be simple or ornate. I have made a set of gate stones from clay that are primitive female images with a notch at the top. The use of gate stones greatly improves the visual aspect of closing and opening a circle. When the broom is across the stones, the gate is closed; when the broom is removed, the gate is open. The gate should be placed at the edge of the circle in a place that will facilitate the ritual activities.

The salt tile is a salt container whose gender is male and whose complement is the water bowl. The salt tile is associated with the element Fire and is used to hold sea salt. Because sea salt represents the male essence of Creation (sperm), the salt tile is often an elongated rectangle or slightly phallic in shape. In ritual, the salt is combined with water (the female essence) to symbolize the union of male and female where the first creation of life took place, the salted waters of the ocean.

The sword has the same attributes as the athame except that, due to its size, it is seen as the complement to the cauldron. It is often preferred over the athame for the casting of the circle, but is a bit too large for many of the other functions of the athame.

The water bowl is a water container whose gender is female and whose complement is the salt dish. The water

Ritual Tool Associations of Creation's Covenant

Magickal Tool	Associated Gender	Associated Element	Associated Quarter	Associated Color	Mate or Complement
Athame	Male	Fire	South	Red	Chalice
Broom	Male	Air	East	Yellow	Gate
Cauldron	Female	Water	West	Blue	Sword
Censer	Male	Air	East	Yellow	Pentacle
Chalice	Female	Water	West	Blue	Athame
Gate	Female	Earth	North	Green	Broom
Pentacle	Female	Earth	North	Green	Censer
Salt tile	Male	Fire	South	Red	Water bowl
Sword	Male	Fire	South	Red	Cauldron
Water bowl	Female	Water	West	Blue	Salt tile

bowl is associated with the element Water and represents the womb of Goddess. During ritual, salt is added to symbolize the male essence of creation (sperm) joining with the womb of Goddess.

Other Tools

Many Wiccans include other tools in their ritual equipment. This is more than acceptable. Additional tools are an expression of the practitioner and are very welcome. Keep in mind that you should only take on new tools as you acquire a need for them. Such tools may include the following:

Anointing bottle: a container with an applicator for scented oils. Some traditions insist that wrists, foreheads, or other body parts be anointed with oil before entering a circle.

Bell (or chime): a device that is sometimes used to signify the beginning and/or ending of a rite.

Boleen: Often confused with the "working knife" (see page 68), the boleen is actually a small hand sickle whose only use is the harvesting of herbs for magickal use. Historical reference seems to indicate that this tool should be made of gold. It seems the ancient Celts harvested mistletoe with a golden sickle, possibly due to the belief that iron is offensive to nature spirits. Because of the great expense of making a gold boleen, other metals are often used, including copper, bronze, and silver. Most of the metals used for the boleen will not hold a sharp edge if used often, which why this tool should never be used for other tasks.

Crown: A crown with a crescent moon is often worn by the High Priestess to symbolize the Goddess, while a crown with antlers is sometimes worn by the High Priest to symbolize the God of the hunt. Other crowns are often used to denote status in specific rites. This is most often with the recreation of the story of the Oak and Holly King. (See page 106.)

Garter: Some traditions hold that the High Priestess should wear a green garter with a silver buckle on it for every coven that she has started.

Thurible: a device other than the censer used for burning similar material. This is most often the burning of parchment, sachets, or herbs. The censer can usually be used for these activities.

Wand (also called Baculum): a tool that has come into the Craft from ceremonial magick roots. Some feel the wand can serve much the same purpose as the athame. *I do not!* Other animals use sticks (wands) to gather food from logs. Humans forge metal to manifest significant changes—try cutting a Goddess image from marble using a stick. I obviously do not think the wand carries the deep associations that the athame does. It has not been used to significantly improve our state of being.

Working knife: a knife that typically has a white handle and is used for physical cutting. It is most often used to carve candles, slice herbs, fashion wood, and perform the tasks that the athame would not be used to perform.

6

The Four Quarters, the Seven Directions, and the Fifth Element

In this chapter we will begin to explore the structure and symbolism of Wiccan ritual. It should be kept in mind that having the perfect temple space no more makes one Wiccan than having the perfect garage makes one a mechanic. What is presented here is what has worked in my tradition. If it doesn't work for you, by all means change it.

The Four Quarters

The Four Quarters (East, South, West, and North) have been called the Four Watchtowers, the Four Winds, and the Four Corners. Although we live in a three-dimensional world, only recently have we moved in more than two dimensions. Where now we send vessels vertically into space and submarines to great depths, until fairly recently we walked, rolled, and sailed along only the surface of this world. The idea of the four directions came from the sky and the earth. The sky provides east and west with the rising and setting of both the sun and the moon. The earth provides north and south with the migration patterns of animals, now believed to be based on magnetic fields. With the simple logic that everything had to come from somewhere, the conclusion was that everything came from at least one of the four directions. From there, attributes were assigned.

Creation's Covenant honors these directions in ritual by inviting their elemental associations. Altars are erected at each quarter. These altars can be small tables, flat rocks, or a simple cloth of color corresponding to each element. They are often decorated with crystals, minerals, and plants in accordance with elemental associations. The four primary ritual tools (athame, chalice, censer, and pentacle) rest upon their respective quarter altars and are brought to the center of the circle during ritual. Each quarter has a gender and elemental association that corresponds to the tool that is placed upon it. Thus, the drawing in of energies from the four quarters is the drawing of male and female forces to the center for the purpose of creation. Exactly what is being created depends on the specific ritual. Some argue that the quarters should only be called once the circle has been cast and that the circle serves to protect those in attendance from the forces they are calling upon. I find it ridiculous that anyone would build a barrier to keep out what one has called in. Consider the circle your home and the quarters your guests. Would you invite guests to your home but refuse to open the door?

In recent times, it has become attractive for each quarter to be called by a member of the group whose astrological sign corresponds to the element being called. This is a nice detail to pay attention to, but it is not necessary and can be very limiting. If you intend to practice with others, remember that the group's ability to relate to each other is far more important than their astrological signs. Some insist that the gender of the quarter be respected by assigning the role of inviting the element to a group member of the corresponding sex. Others feel that the opposite sex should be used because opposites attract. Again, I think the choice of who does the inviting is less important than group dynamics. I see no harm in either of these practices except that they are limiting.

This would be a good time to draw a distinction between gender and sex for the purpose of explanation in this book. I have found the following to effectively convey what I seek to express: An object has gender, as in the gender of an athame is male. People have sex. The sex that we call male is actually a fusion of the gender female and the gender male with emphasis on the gender male. The inverse is true for the sex that we call female. While it is preferable that a male hold the athame and a woman hold the chalice during the symbolic Great Rite, it is not necessary.

East

The East Quarter is associated with the element Air. Its gender is male and its complement is the element Earth. Planetary associations with this quarter are Mercury, Venus, and Uranus. The East is from whence we draw logical thought and is the source our rational mind. It is our very breath and the breath of all living things. At our first breath, it becomes the primary element of our birth.

In Creation's Covenant, the forces of the East are honored with an altar erected in the easternmost point of the ritual area. This altar is most often painted or covered with yellow fabric. It is where the censer and incense rest prior to ritual and where these items are returned during the closing of ritual. A yellow candle should be available to honor this quarter.

South

The South Quarter is associated with the element Fire. Its gender is male and its complement is the element Water. Planetary associations with this quarter are Mars, Sun, and Jupiter. The South is from whence we draw emotion and is the source of emotional sensation. It is the driving force behind our soul, our spirit, and the spirit of all living things. It is the primary element of our youth.

In Creation's Covenant, the forces of the South are honored with an altar erected in the southernmost point of the ritual area. This altar is most often painted or covered with red fabric. It is where the athame (and sword if one is used) rest prior to ritual and where these items are returned during the closing of ritual. A red candle should be available to honor this quarter.

West

The West Quarter is associated with the element Water. Its gender is female and its complement is the element Fire. Planetary associations with this quarter are Moon, Pluto, and Neptune. The West is from whence we draw intuition and is the source of psychic sensation. It is our life's blood and the life's blood of all living things. It is the primary element of our midlife.

In Creation's Covenant, the forces of the West are honored with an altar erected in the westernmost point of the ritual area. This altar is most often painted or covered with blue fabric. It is where the chalice rests prior to ritual and where it is returned during the closing of ritual. A blue candle should be available to honor this quarter.

North

The North Quarter is associated with the element Earth. Its gender is female and its complement is the element Air. Planetary associations with this quarter are Venus, Mercury, and Saturn. The North is from whence we draw our firm connection to the physical and is the source of the desire for physical sensation. It is our body and the body of all living things. It is the primary element of our later years and where we will return in our death.

In Creation's Covenant, the forces of the North are honored with an altar erected in the northern-most point of the ritual area. This altar is most often painted or covered with green fabric. It is where the pentacle rests prior to ritual and where these items are returned during the closing of ritual. A green candle should be available to honor this quarter.

The Seven Directions

When most people think of directions, they recognize only the first four: north, south, east, and west. This would be fine if we were living in a two-dimensional world, but in our world, there are three additional directions: above, below, and center. Indeed, many Wiccans do not realize that in their rites they are honoring the other three. All Wiccans honor the Lord or God of Wicca (Father Sky) and Lady or Goddess of Wicca (Mother Earth). The names may vary; indeed, even the associations with Earth and Sky may not be observed. But the two main forces that are being honored are that of male and female.

Above is the expression of all things male. It is rain and sun reaching downward for union with vegetation and the driving force of change, especially sudden change. It is the force that calls the sky to reach down to the mountains and the lightning that reached down to a primordial ocean to conceive the first life.

Below is the expression of all things female. It is vegetation reaching upward for the union of rain and sun and the force that calls the mountains to reach up to the sky. It is the primordial ocean that welcomed lightning to conceive the first life.

The final direction is center. Although this direction is not always immediately recognized, it is as valid as any other. Without center, it would not be possible to define a three-dimensional space. Center is the direction of creation. It is where Air meets Earth, Fire meets Water, Lord meets Lady, and male meets female. It is the point of conception and the point of birth.

These three additional directions or forces are honored at the main altar. This altar is typically larger than the quarter altars and should be placed in the center of the working area. It can be of any shape. A square table will do, although round seems to be preferred. I have found that rectangular seems to work best for me. This altar is the union place of the elements. It is the marital bed of the Lord and Lady. To this altar is brought both athame, the central male symbol, and chalice, the central female symbol, to be joined in the ritual creation of life.

Although the center altar is one table, it is actually three altars. One-third of the altar is dedicated to Goddess (below), one-third to God (above), and one-third to the union of God and Goddess which is Life (center). Many Wiccans place the altar facing east then divide the altar with Goddess on the left or north side, God on the right or south side, and Life at center. Because north has a female gender and south has a male gender, this system is appropriate, but what of south and west? To create more balance, Creation's Covenant places the main altar in the center and aligns the male portion towards the southeast and the female portion northwest.

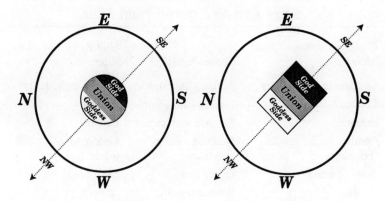

Altar alignment with both rectangular and round altars

Some Neo-Pagan traditions represent a similar concept with the World Tree. The roots are grounded in the earth, the branches reach for the sky, and the trunk (center) is present in the here and now. Additional associations can be made to the past and future meeting in the present. Some physicists now think there may be as many as twenty-six dimensions, so there is definitely room to expand on the concept of forces and directions meeting at center.

A candle representing the male forces should be placed on the God side of the altar as well as a candle for the female forces on the Goddess side. Gender-specific candles can be found at most Neo-Pagan shops and through mail order suppliers. These candles most often appear in the image of an anatomically correct male and female, however, any candle will do. It is best that these candles be of different colors or shades of the same color. I prefer black and white. A bottle, pitcher, or vase of water should be placed on the Goddess side of the altar, an empty bowl in the center of the altar, and a dish of sea salt on the God side. It is an excellent idea to hide matches or a lighter somewhere in the ritual space in case you forget. Some even advocate taping a lighter to the underside of the altar.

Suggested Use of the Main Altar

Goddess Portion of Main Altar	Center Portion	God Portion of Main Altar
Goddess image/statuary*	Statuary of couples*	God image/statuary*
Chalice	Chalice with athame	Athame
Pentacle	Pentacle with censer	Censer
Gender-specific candle (Female)*	Wedding candles*	Gender-specific candle (Male)*
Bowl of water	Empty bowl	Bowl of salt
Seashell*	White candle	Antler*
Drink (wine/juice)		Food (cakes/breads)*
Green candle (Earth)		Yellow candle (Air)
Blue candle (Water)		Red candle (Fire)

*Denotes items that are optional

It is most appropriate for symbols of the Lord and Lady to be found on the main altar. If semiprecious stones, flowers, and herbs are used to decorate the main altar, their location on the altar should follow the gender of these items. As tools are brought to the main altar from the quarter altars, they should be placed appropriately during the ritual.

Please note that the candles used to honor the Four Quarters are placed on the main altar according to their gender associations.

The Fifth Element

The fifth element is what draws the first four elements together. It is the driving force to unite, live, create, and procreate. The fifth element is what each of us carries into ritual and is the cause of the structure of the ritual itself. It is the driving force that brings together athame to chalice, man to woman. It is also the result of these unions, life.

The Pentagram   **Man as Microcosm**

Pentagram with five elements and Man as Microcosm

It is the spark within each living thing that says that life is good. It is what makes us smile and laugh. It is the force that drives a rabbit to run from a fox. It is also called Akasha or Spirit.

Consider the creation of pottery. Earth is moistened with water. The mixture is shaped, then fused with fire and cooled with air. Each of the four elements was used to create form and function, sometimes even beauty. But if we eliminate the creative force within the potter, what would we have other than mud?

The fifth element is also the driving force that inspires the fox to chase after the rabbit. It is what causes us to frown and cry. The fifth element can be seen as the driving force to divide, kill, and destroy. For light to exist, there must be darkness. For summer, there must be winter. For warmth, there must be cold. For life, there must be death. This is the cycle of life. The fifth element is the force that drives that cycle.

This concept is represented in the most common Wiccan symbol, the pentagram. Not to be confused with the pentacle, which is a ritual device that represents the earth, the pentagram is a five-pointed star within a circle. The four lower points represent the first four elements. There is some argument over which point is which. What no one seems to argue is that the fifth element is placed on top to crown the others. This significance shows that the fifth element is supreme. The circle reminds us that all are one, that each of the elements is used to create the whole. The pentagram is also the symbol of humanity. This can be seen as the man in the wheel.

Note: Creation's Covenant assigns the four lower elements this way for two reasons. First, they are in the order in which they are found in Wiccan ritual at the quarters. Second, because this places the heavier elements on the bottom and the lighter elements on the top, this seems to make sense.

7

Ritual and the Building of a Wiccan Temple

In this chapter we will cover the opening and the closing of ritual in Creation's Covenant. What goes on in between is the intent, the purpose of the rite. For a celebration of the Sabbat, you will find guidelines and suggestions in chapter 8. Complete rituals can be found in the attached Book of Shadows (chapter 12).

What Is Ritual?

While speaking on what seems to have become my annual October chat on a local talk radio show, a caller asked if I could describe the "ritual of skyclad." My immediate response was to say that to the best of my knowledge there was no "ritual of skyclad." I informed the caller that the term *skyclad* means to be naked or clad only by the sky. While some prefer to practice this way, I was unaware of any ritual written specifically to become naked. During a commercial break, I reconsidered my answer. The word *ritual* describes an action that is repeated—it doesn't require a formal religious significance. After the commercial was over, I announced that I do have a personal "ritual of skyclad." Although I don't always follow it exactly, first I take off my shoes, then my socks. You can figure out the rest. More often than not, the ritual is concluded with a hot shower or bath.

The word ritual typically stirs up thoughts of sombei ceremonies and rites dedicated to long-forgotten Gods. Incense is always thought to be burning in the background, while black-clad leaders banter in ancient languages. A level of fear is heavy in the air. If this is what you are looking for, stop reading this book, close its covers, and rent a video. Wicca celebrates life and commemorates the natural cycles of living with its rituals. As such, these celebrations are joyous occasions filled with song and wine.

Why Conduct Ritual?

I am amazed by the number of things people do without knowing why they do them. When it comes to matters which have a profound impact on our lives, it is best to conduct ourselves with clear intent. Know what you are doing and why.

Many Wiccans believe they conduct rituals to praise the Lord and Lady. Remember that ritual is an activity that is repeated again and again. Are we to believe that the Lord and Lady would not accept our praise in a different format each time? Do your parents get upset when you give them a different present every birthday or Yule?

All cultures have rituals for the same purpose—to remember. Repetition assists memorization. Just as a student creates study rituals to improve grades, Wiccans create and perform rituals to improve their understanding of and relationship with the Lord and Lady and all they have created. By starting ritual in the East, one develops a sense of where East is. We begin to remember where East is even when we are not in a ritual. By celebrating the solar and lunar events, one becomes attuned to the celestial cycles. We begin to remember where they are on the wheel of the year. By marking the cross quarters, one becomes synchronous with the earth. We begin to remember that we are part of the earth.

The Wiccan gives praise to his Lord and Lady with every movement, with every thought, with every dream and aspiration. The very living of life is the praise of life. Our love for the Lord and Lady is not confined to ritual. We continue the relationship in the home, in public, in the workplace. As all things are of God and Goddess, all actions are interactions with God and Goddess. There is no exception. Even in death, we are celebrating the natural conclusion to this life. All things are sacred.

It is said that imitation is the highest form of flattery. This is what Wiccan rituals are. They are sacred plays that complement and commemorate the life force. They affirm that the cycles of life are good and celebrate life by imitating life. Where a circle is cast, a home is built. Where an athame is joined with a chalice, a magickal child is conceived. It is easy to see how, since our lives are not lived entirely within our homes, our praise and rituals need not always be in the confines of a cast circle. However, just as in our homes, the cast circle is often where we feel most comfortable.

Who Are the Ritual Leaders and Why?

Typically, Wiccan ritual is lead by a Priest and a Priestess. Together, the Priest and Priestess represent deity in Wiccan rites. They are seen as the earthly representation of God and Goddess.

Some Wiccan groups (often called covens) are started when a Priest or Priestess leaves his or her original coven and births a new one. He or she brings the traditions of his or her former coven into this new coven. This happens most often in covens that enforce a degree system. Once the final degree of initiation is reached, the Priest or Priestess is given the authority to start a new branch of the root tradition. The Priest or Priestess of these types of covens are often authoritarian in the same way as many college professors. If you do not like the way they teach, you are always welcome to leave, but you may not make claim to their tradition in the same way you may not take credit for the class.

Most often, a Priest or Priestess will form a coven around the teachings he or she has received from books, generally because there seem to be a great many more books (not titles) on Wicca than there are Wiccan covens. Although some Wiccans may frown upon this practice, I think that the ability of a Priest or Priestess to serve his or her coven can be determined by his or her own actions, not necessarily by his or her accreditations. In the same way a coach can be judged by the performance of his team, the leaders of a coven can be judged by the performance of that coven.

Some groups start without a clear sense of leadership. Like minds tend to attract one another. A Priest and Priestess are then selected from the membership. This is done by vote, consensus, or competition of some sort. Sometimes it is agreed that the Priest and Priestess shall serve for only a set period of time; sometimes this selection is made for each ritual.

Creation's Covenant is different from most traditions in the way that we form groups. We consider members of our tradition to be members of our extended family. What most Wiccans call a coven, we call a household. Members of a particular household are considered members of the immediate family of all other members of that particular household. Households form the way family households form: by birth, adoption, friendship, and marriage.

In a Creation's Covenant ritual, the Priest and Priestess are simply the host and hostess of the household and the household is built around their hospitality. If a member of that household is unsatisfied with the hospitality, he or she is welcome to form his or her own household, join another household in the tradition, practice as a solitary, or leave the tradition entirely. The choice is entirely his or hers. He or she is welcome to continue as a member of our tradition (extended family), just not as one of the particular household that was left. Indeed, many members of this tradition have not aligned with a particular household and practice very contentedly as solitaries.

The Priest (host) and Priestess (hostess) only guide the household in rituals. They do not rule the rites or anyone in attendance at the rites. Each member of our tradition is his or her own master.

Preparing the Wiccan Temple

The Foundation Explained

All structures need a good foundation and the temple is no exception. The first step in building the temple is deciding where it will be placed. This will change from season to season and celebration to celebration. If you choose a location and find too many drawbacks, change the location. Selecting sacred space is not simply a matter of what feels right is right—mundane concerns such as temperature and weather need to be addressed. In general, it's preferable that winter rites be conducted indoors and summer rites outdoors. Unless there is clear reason to move a ritual, such as a storm threat, try to keep all rites in the same location. This forms a pattern and increases participation. Remember that in this matter, although what feels right is not necessarily right, what feels wrong is always wrong.

To prepare the foundation for your temple, clear the area of anything not involved in the ritual. If outdoors, remove deadfall wood, rocks, and other items one might trip over. Do not remove living vegetation indiscriminately. Sure, you can mow your lawn if it is necessary, but hacking down living things to create an area in which to praise life is defeating your goal before you begin. If the area is overgrown and inhospitable to your purposes, consider it divine intervention. Find a different location. If you have an unused room indoors, devote that room as a shrine. If you want to practice indoors but do not have the permanent space to commit, improvise. Try to keep all ritual items in the same location to make setting up easy. I have a friend who uses an army footlocker as his main altar and color-coded pieces of cloth as his quarter altars. When he is finished, everything is placed in the footlocker except the pentacle, which he hangs over the door to his home as a protective talisman.

Once the location is determined and the peripheral clearing has been concluded, it should be made ready on both a physical and spiritual plane. A good way to cleanse the circle both physically and spiritually is to use the broom or besom. Starting at the center, sweep outward in a counterclockwise spiral to a point outside of the boundaries your circle will create. Moving counterclockwise is the act of casting out. As you sweep, visualize any undesired energies being swept away with the dust. For spiritual cleansing it is not necessary for the bristles of the broom to actually contact the ground or floor, but why not clean the physical site as well? If your broom is laced with small bells, the noise made by sweeping is generally thought to scare away baneful entities.

Other ways of spiritually cleansing the circle are numerous. I have found that the Native American custom of smudging works well. Smudge sticks are bundles of sage and sometimes cedar and lavender. To perform the smudging, light the large end of the stick, allow it to burn for a few moments, then snuff the flame but allow the bundle to smolder. You may have to fan the smoldering end to keep it burning. Start at the center of the circle and move outward as you did with the broom, fanning smoke so that it fills the air. Note, however, that sage smoke will set off almost any smoke detector. Burning sage also tends to attract undue attention since when burned, it is often confused with the smell of burning marijuana. With the area prepared and altars arranged as discussed in the previous chapter, the temple is ready to be constructed.

The Temple Explained

Wiccans do not need a building to practice their rites; the magick circle is their temple. Because everyone who enters circle with you is either your brother, sister, or honored guest, consider the temple your home. It is the place you are going to invite your Mother Goddess and Father God to visit. Remember that as we are natural creatures, the homes that we build should also be natural.

The circle in Wiccan ritual is an enclosure. Enclosures can be historically documented time and time again. Where we have built, we have built walls. Where we have built walls, we have built enclosures to protect us against harmful forces. Castles and forts have been erected to stave off invading armies, but they have also been built for comfort. They retain heat in the winter and define our realm. Wolves and other animals will leave scent in a circle around their domain to let other animals know where their territory ends. The Wiccan does not view the circle as a territorial warning; instead, the circle is the defining parameter of outside influence. It is shelter from forces that do not belong within the celebration. If there are forces and energies that you fear, simply do not invite them in.

The size of the circle is dependent on the number of people in attendance as well as the activities that will take place. I have found that in a larger group, if everyone can extend their arms and touch the hand of the person next to them, the size is perfect. Everything within this circle of people is the working space. With smaller groups and solitary practitioners, the circle size should be dictated by the activities to be conducted within it. The circle is sometimes marked with chalk, flowers, herbs, a cord, or other device, but marking the circle is not a very common practice, though it can improve atmosphere. If you are going to mark the circle, choose a device that has associations with the purpose of the ritual.

Before the Ritual

The altars and ritual space are made ready before the ritual begins. In Creation's Covenant, the altars are arranged and placed as previously discussed. The structure of Wicca is dissimilar from traditional Western religions in regard to group involvement—Wiccan services are for participants, not spectators. Have participants meet before the ritual to help with the preparations. This helps to gather the group and lessen the impact of late arrivals since if someone arrives late, they are more likely to miss the preparation than the actual rite. Further, this brings the group together at a central point prior to the rite so that if a member encounters transportation problems, other group members can lend a hand.

The Challenge

Wiccan ritual must always begin with an assurance that all who are to be involved are present by their own free will. This often takes the form of the challenge. I have heard some truly poetic challenges, but all that is necessary is to ask someone, "Are you here by your own free will?" This challenge is often received at sword- or knifepoint, but this really is not necessary and can be very disconcerting. One of the most beautiful and effective challenges I have heard came from the young daughter of the ritual organizers at our local Covenant of Universal Unitarian Pagans. It took the form of a question: "How do you enter this circle?" The answer had been prearranged earlier: "In perfect love and perfect trust." Although it is common to prearrange the answer to the challenge, I would advise you not to do so. I think that it is often like asking the participants to lie. If the answers are honest and from the heart, no two people will answer in the same way. This is especially true in public rituals. Expecting "perfect love and perfect trust" from perfect strangers is a little more than I would request. If it is a solitary who is practicing, the challenge may take the form of a proclamation, which is best spoken outloud. "I enter this circle of my own free will." If it is a small group, arrange the group in a circle where the ritual will take place. Have the ritual organizers or Priest and Priestess challenge each other, then issue the challenge to each individual. If possible, the Priest should ask the women and the Priestess should ask the men. If it is a large group, one mass challenge inviting those who are not present by their own free will to leave should be spoken: "If you are here by your own free will, please join us in our rite. If you are not, please leave now, for the ceremony is about to begin."

The gesture of the Wiccan cross (see page 38) is then given by either the Priest or Priestess. If there are people present who are likely not to understand the gesture, it should be explained. Any member of the circle who accepts the symbolism of the gesture should return the Wiccan cross as discussed previously. Solitary practitioners should perform the Wiccan cross as if they were responding to the gesture being given to them by the Lord and Lady.

Lighting the Work Candle

After the challenge is given but before the circle is cast, the work candle is lit. Traditionally, all candles, incense, and other combustibles should be lit from this candle. This practice comes from the belief that sulfur, which is found in many matches, is a banishing agent. This would make striking a match in the confines of a circle baneful if your intent is not to banish. If you choose to follow this tradition, I suggest lighting at least two work candles and tap-ing a lighter under the main altar. Be aware that avoiding sulfur inside a closed circle is difficult because many incenses and charcoals contain a small amount. If you really want leave the sulfur out of your rites, use the type of incense that burns over charcoal and light your charcoal at the same time the work candle is lit. The sulfur that charcoal typically contains will quickly burn away. It will also give the charcoal time to get hot before adding the incense later.

Casting the Circle

When a group is gathered in a circle and the challenge given, some feel that the circle is already cast as it is sometimes felt that the presence of those in attendance is what forms the circle. I prefer the more theatrical approach, where a circle is cast a few feet outside of the circle of people. This is most often done with an athame or sword. Go to the Fire (South Quarter) altar and lift the athame or sword, move clockwise to the just beyond the Air (East Quarter) altar, starting where the day starts. For the first casting of the circle, the athame is pointed at the ground. Visualize a great energy entering the body from above and leaving the body through the hands and being directed by the athame into the ground. If in a group setting, instruct the group to visualize the casting of the circle downward, through the earth and forming a half circle beneath the ritual space. Either sex can cast the first circle, but it is most appropriate for a male to cast the downward circle because it is God's energy being channeled. Chanting during the casting of the circle is a good way to raise energy: "Circle strong and circle bright! Merry meet, enjoy the night!" is one of my favorites. The first casting of the circle moves from just beyond the Air altar, clockwise back to the starting point, while visualizing the circle as a half sphere moving beneath the earth. After the first casting of the circle, the athame is returned to the Fire altar.

Many Wiccans consider the circle now cast. Although the tool is directed downward, they visualize the sphere forming in both directions. Rather than simply stopping here,

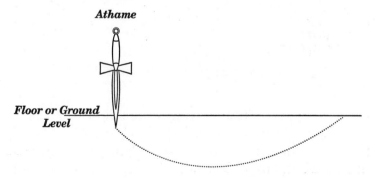

Athame

Floor or <u>Ground</u> Level

First casting of the circle (downward)

Creation's Covenant prefers to consider the casting of the circle the first opportunity to fuse male and female energy.

The first casting of the circle is the drawing of male energy from above (Father Sky) and directing it to below (Mother Earth). The second casting of the circle is the drawing of female energy from below (Mother Earth) and directing it to above (Father Sky). This casting of the circle follows the same method of the first except that the athame is pointed upward and the visualization is of the energy swelling from below, entering the body at the feet, and leaving through the athame directed upward to form a half sphere arched over the circle. Either sex can cast the second circle, however, it is more appropriate for this circle to be cast by a female because it is Goddess's energy that is being channeled. The athame is then returned to the Fire altar. The casting of the circle is now complete.

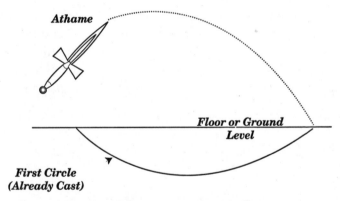

First casting of the circle (upward)

An Offering to the Outsiders

I am not entirely sure where this practice originated. I was first introduced to it through the liturgy of an organization called "Ar nDraiocht Fein" a Gaelic term which the ADF reports to mean "our own Druidry" but which actually translates to "our own magick." You see, there is no word in Gaelic for Druid. The outsiders offering involves leaving the circle to make an offering to the outsiders, who represent the forces that might trouble your rite. They are those who once challenged the Gods and Goddesses and lost. The offering is made to appease them, not to invite them.

Each of us has a portion of the outsiders within our bodies. These destructive forces can include greed, bigotry, jealousy, and other baneful emotions or thoughts. The outsider offering is a way of symbolically removing these forces from ourselves for the rite. With repetition, perhaps they will remain outside our psyche as well.

The way I typically conduct an outsider offering is to explain the practice to everyone in circle and ask them to visualize the outsiders within themself leaving the body and forming a sphere that rests on the palms of their extended hands. I then go to each person and ask them to empty their negative energy (outsiders) into a box which I created specifically for this purpose. My outsider box is dark stained-glass on the outside with a completely mirrored inside, created to trap the energy. When dealing with truly baneful energies and thoughts, this box may be sealed and stored indefinitely.

Be creative with the outsider offering. A close friend came up with a great one. She fills a large chalice with water. A vessel with a large mouth is left empty. The water-filled chalice is given to each member by the Priestess. A mouthful is taken and swished around the mouth. The water is then spit into the empty container. As you spit, visualize the negative forces leaving with the water.

Whatever the method you use, when everyone has gotten rid of their personal outsiders, the Priest carries the outsiders from within through the gate to the outside of the circle. After he returns, the Priestess prepares a plate (simple bread will do) and glass (the ritual wine is best) for the offering. She leaves the circle through the gate and places the offering outside the circle. "This is an offering for the outsiders," she says. "This is for those who would do us harm. It is made that you will trouble us not." The Priestess returns and the gate is closed.

This is a new practice to Creation's Covenant, but I like it and it seems to work well. Play with the roles. Write your own words. If you use the gargle and spit method, try boiling mint in the water, especially during Bealtaine and other rites where kissing might occur.

Calling Quarters: The Union of Air and Earth

Take the green candle from the Goddess side of the altar. Light the candle from the work candle and bring it to the Earth (West Quarter) altar. At this point, invite the element Earth to join the rite: "I invite the element Earth, that which is my body and the body of all here to attend our rite." Leave the candle atop the Earth altar. Bring the pentacle to the main altar, and as you bring it to center announce: "Here I bring Earth to the center of this rite." Place the pentacle in the center section of the altar.

Light the yellow candle from the work candle, then bring it to the Air (East Quarter) altar. At this point, invite the element Air to join the rite: "I invite the element Air, the breath of all things, that which is my breath and the breath of all here to attend our rite." If the incense or charcoal is not already lit, ignite it now from the Air candle. If you're using charcoal and you have already lit it, add the incense at this point. Leave the candle on the Air altar. Place the incense in the censer and bring the censer to the main altar. As you bring it to center, announce: "Here I bring Air to the center of this rite." Place the censer on top of the pentacle.

In a group that contains both sexes, it is preferred that a female invite Earth, a male invite Air, and that the tools are brought to the center altar at the same time. If practicing as a solitary, you should first invite Earth and then Air. This way the pentacle arrives at the center altar before the hot censer.

Lift the pentacle with the censer atop it and affirm the symbolism to all in attendance: "This is the union of Air and Earth, Male and Female." If you wish to affirm the meaning of the pentacle and censer, feel free to do so. Then use the pentacle with the censer atop and smudge the circle and the practitioners. This is done by bringing the pentacle and censer to the easternmost point in the circle and then walking clockwise within the circle of people. Waft the rising smoke towards those in attendance for purification and to attune them to the rite. Once you have made a full circle, return the censer and pentacle to the center section of the altar, leaving them united. The first two quarters have now been called.

Calling Quarters: The Union of Fire and Water

Take the red candle from the God side of the altar. Light the candle from the work candle and bring it to the Fire (South Quarter) altar. Invite the element Fire to join the rite: "I invite the element Fire, that which is my spirit and the spirit of all here to attend our rite." Leave the candle atop the Fire altar. Take the athame to the main altar, as you bring it to the main altar, announce: "Here I bring Fire to the center of this rite."

Take the blue candle from the Goddess side of the altar. Light the candle from the work candle and bring it to the Water (West Quarter) altar. Invite the element Water to join the rite: "I invite the element Water, the blood of all things, that which is my blood and the blood of all here to attend our rite." Place the candle on the Water altar. Bring the chalice to the main altar and fill it with water if you have not already. As you bring it to the main altar, announce: "Here I bring Water to the center of this rite."

In a group that contains both sexes, it is preferred that a male invite Fire and bring the athame to center and a female invite Water and bring the chalice to center. The female holds the chalice at waist level. The male takes the tile or dish of salt from the God side of the altar and measures three portions with the athame into the chalice. The athame and salt are returned to the God side of the altar. The salted water is poured from the chalice to the dish in the center of the altar and the empty chalice is placed on the Goddess side of the altar. If practicing as a solitary, you should invite Fire first to maintain balance. (When the last two elements were called, a female element was invited first.)

Lift the dish of salted water and affirm the symbolism to all in attendance: "This is the union of Fire and Water, it is spirit and blood." If you wish to affirm the meaning of the salt as the spark of life provided by our Lord blending with water which is the womb of our Lady, feel free to do so. The salted water is then used to sprinkle the circle and the practitioners. This is done by bringing the salted water to the easternmost point in the circle and then walking clockwise within the circle of people, lightly sprinkling those in attendance with the fingers for purification. Once you have made a full circle, return the dish of salted water to the center section of the altar, leaving them united. The second two quarters have now been called.

Inviting Deity and the Great Rite

The exact words for inviting the Lord and Lady should come from the heart and correspond to the purpose of the rite. This does not mean that the words cannot be written and rehearsed; however, they should at minimum be written and rehearsed by the one to invite each. A solitary practitioner would invite both Lord and Lady as honored guests to be welcomed in the circle. In the case of a group containing both men and women, the Priest welcomes Goddess to the rite, inviting the Priestess to become his Lady and the Priestess welcomes God to the rite, inviting the Priest to become her Lord. Wine or fruit juice is poured into the chalice by the Priestess, who holds the chalice at waist level. The Priest lifts the athame and holds it over the chalice with the point down. In words similar to those below, the symbolism of lowering the athame into the chalice is spoken as the athame is descends into the chalice: "The union of the athame to the chalice is the union of man to woman, for the fulfillment of both, and the creation of what we hold most dear: life itself. This is our most holy of rites."

The act of joining athame and chalice is referred to as the symbolic Great Rite. There is absolutely no rule or law which forbids the actual Great Rite, or the sexual union of the Priest and Priestess, to occur at this point in ritual. With the great amount of sexual repression in our culture, a working couple (without a coven) will likely benefit greatly from making their sexual union sacred. However, in our culture, it is ill-advised to do so publicly or even within the sanctity of a coven unless you welcome ridicule.

The wine is now shared with all in attendance. The wine is the life force that is the result of the union of God and Goddess. The building of the temple is complete. What follows depends on the purpose of the ritual.

Closing the Temple

Closing the temple follows the reverse order of opening. If you are a solitary practitioner, thank the Lord and Lady for attending in your own words. If a Priest and Priestess have invited each other to become deity, the Priestess thanks the Priest for becoming her Lord and the Priest thanks and Priestess for becoming his Lady. If the Priest and Priestess are lovers, it is appropriate for each to welcome the other to continue in the role of their deity:

Priest: "I thank my Goddess for being present in my partner for this rite. Go if you must, remain if you will. I will love and honor you forever."

Priestess: "I thank my God for being present in my partner for this rite. Go if you must, remain if you will. I will love and honor you forever."

Before returning the chalice to the Water altar and the athame to the Fire altar, it should be affirmed in similar words that: "Once again we separate athame and chalice, male and female, that we might again know the joy of their union." The person who invited the element Water should return the chalice to the Water altar, then thank the element and invite it to "Go if you must, but stay if you will." He or she then brings the blue candle back to the center and places it on the Goddess side of the altar. The athame should be returned to the Fire altar in the same manner. Thank the element Fire in similar words and return the red candle to the God side of the main altar.

Before returning the censer to the Air altar and the pentacle to the Earth altar, it should be affirmed in similar words that: "Once again we separate censer and pentacle, male and female, that we might again know the joy of their union." The person who invited Air should then return the censer to the Air altar, and thank the element Air with similar words: "Go if you must, but stay if you will." That person should bring the yellow candle to the main altar and place it on the God side of the altar. The pentacle should be returned to the Earth altar in the same way, and the element Earth should be thanked in similar words. The green candle is returned to the Goddess side of the main altar.

The circle is opened in the same way it was closed (cast), by tracing it with the athame or sword. Again this is done by starting in the east and moving full circle from the easternmost point back again to the easternmost point. This is done by the same people who cast the circle, only in reverse order and moving counterclockwise. As this is done, visualize the energy that was used to cast the circle reentering the athame or sword and being stored for the next rite. A good chant for opening the circle is: "The circle is open, but never broken." Once the circle has been opened, the temple is closed with the following chant: "Merry meet, merry part, and merry meet again!"

8

Sabbats and the Wheel of the Year: Days of Celebration

All religions have days of celebration and Wicca is no exception. These holidays are most commonly referred to as the sabbats, from the French word *s'ebattre*, which means to rejoice, frolic, and revel. That is exactly what these days are: times to celebrate life and to rejoice in what the year has given us at each point. This chapter will discuss each sabbat and how it is celebrated. The current specific rites of Creation's Covenant can be found in the Book of Shadows (chapter 12).

There are a total of eight sabbats each year. Four are on the natural four quarters of the solar year, marked by the two solstices and the two equinoxes. The other four are on the points halfway between the quarters. Because nature is not stagnant, the exact dates of the sabbats cannot be set. They change from year to year with the solstices and the equinoxes. Modern authors have attempted to exact these dates, but because they are attempting to make static what is dynamic, these authors do not always agree. The following dates were taken from *Eight Sabbats for Witches* by the Farrars, *The Sabbats* by Edain McCoy, and *Wicca: A Guide for the Solitary Practitioner* by Scott Cunningham:

Sabbat	Farrar	McCoy	Cunningham
Samhain	Oct. 31	Oct. 31	Oct. 31
Winter Solstice	Dec. 22	Dec. 22	Dec. 21
Imbolc	Feb. 2	Feb. 2	Feb. 2
Spring Equinox	Mar. 21	Mar. 22	Mar. 21
Bealtaine	Apr. 30	May 1	Apr. 30
Summer Solstice	June 22	June 22	June 21
Lughnasadh	July 31	Aug. 1 or 2	Aug. 1
Autumn Equinox	Sept. 21	Sept. 22	Sept. 21

To find the date of each sabbat, consider a circle to be the whole of the year. Divide the circle in half from top to bottom. The point at the top is the Winter Solstice and the point at the bottom is the Summer Solstice. These dates can be found on almost every calendar. Next, draw a line horizontally to split the circle into quarters. The point where this line intersects the circle at the left is the Autumn Equinox and at the right is the Spring Equinox. Lastly, add two more lines dividing the quarters into eighths. You have just drawn the wheel of the year.

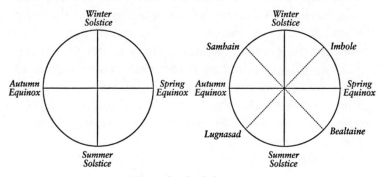

The wheel of the year

Sabbat Name	*Location on the Wheel/Descriptive Date*
Samhain	Midpoint between Autumn Equinox and Winter Solstice
Winter Solstice	On the first day of winter
Imbolc	Midpoint between Winter Solstice and Spring Equinox
Spring Equinox	On the first day of spring
Bealtaine	Midpoint between Spring Equinox and Summer Solstice
Summer Solstice	On the first day of summer
Lughnasadh	Midpoint between Summer Solstice and Autumn Equinox
Autumn Equinox	On the first day of autumn

If it is not possible for you to celebrate these events on the date of their occurrence, it is best to mark the actual date in a small way but schedule the full rite when you can. Due to work and the other limitations of our modern world, my household uses the following guidelines. If the actual date of the event falls on a Saturday, it is always celebrated on that date. If the date is any other day of the week, we celebrate on the Saturday that falls *before* the sabbat. The one exception to this rule is that we have given into the popular dictates when it comes to Samhain, which we always celebrate twice. Our private celebration always occurs on the actual date (halfway between the Autumn Equinox and the Winter Solstice), but our public celebration, the Real Witches' Ball, is celebrated on the weekend of October 31, if the 31st falls on a weekend. If not, the ball is held on the Saturday preceding October 31. We considered other more realistic dates for the ball, but fighting the popular belief that Samhain (a.k.a. Halloween) occurs on October 31 would be pointless. Besides, what better time to demonstrate what *real* Witchcraft is all about?

Celebration days can be classified as quarter days and cross-quarter days. The quarter days are the celebrations of the solstices and equinoxes. They are called the quarter days because they are the points that slice the solar year into quarters. They are also called the Lesser Sabbats. Cross-quarter days fall in between the quarter days. They are also known as the Greater Sabbats. These days are referred to in this way because Gardner based much of his structure on the Celts and the Celts seem to have felt that cross-quarter days were more important than the quarter days. Creation's Covenant makes no such associations. We feel that continuing to associate the sabbats with a cultural bias only serves to perpetuate stagnation, so we refer to the sabbats simply as quarter days and cross-quarter days.

To further prevent cultural bias, we call the quarter days by the description of what they are. Rather than calling Winter Solstice Yule, we simply call it Winter Solstice. The cross-quarter days will retain their Celtic names until we can find something better. Let's face it, it is easy to call Winter Solstice what it is but to call Samhain "the day that falls in between Autumn Equinox and Winter Solstice" just takes too much effort.

Samhain: A Cross-Quarter Day

ASSOCIATED GEMS: Obsidian, onyx, and carnelian
ASSOCIATED FOODS: Apples, squash, fresh meat, and
   ancestral favorites
ASSOCIATED SPICES AND HERBS: Allspice, catnip, and sage
ALSO KNOWN AS: All Hallow's Eve, All Saint's Eve, Calan
   Gaeaf, Celtic New Year, Day of the Dead, Feast of
   Spirits, Hallowmas, Martinmas, Samonios, Samhuinn,
   Santos, and Third Harvest

This sabbat actually falls between the Autumn Equinox and the Winter Solstice, but is almost exclusively observed on October 31. Although Hollywood has created the false belief that Samhain is the name of the Celtic God of Death, one would be hard-pressed to substantiate this. Not only is that God nonexistent in Celtic lore, he's missing from the religious lore of all people. The closest reference I have been able to find is "Samana," who is reported by Edain McCoy in *The Sabbats* to be an Aryan God of death. Samhain is the word the Celts used to note their celebration of the end of summer and the birth of a new year, hence my belief that Samhain has its roots in the Gaelic words "sam" meaning summer and "fuin" meaning end.

Samhain is a time of endings. Perhaps no deity image is more associated with Samhain than the Crone aspect of the Triple Goddess. The elder stages of life are revered with images of Hecate and Cerridwen, the dark mothers. From these sacred visions come those common distorted images of haglike green Witches with long wart-crowned noses. Most Wiccans find these images as offensive as an African American might find a black-face comedy routine.

Samhain marks the end of the harvest. According to some, taking in crops after Samhain will be punished with bad luck in the year to come. Samhain is also known as the Blood Harvest or the Blood Feast. In times of old, the crop yield determined the amount of grain that could be stored to feed livestock through the winter. If the harvest fell short, the animals that would otherwise starve were slaughtered. Because grain and other vegetable products could be stored easily but meat could not, great amounts of the meat had to be consumed directly after the slaughter so that it would not go to waste. Although this practice is not conducted widely in the United States, it is still common for Samhain feasts to include large amounts of fresh meat. Fortunately for those of us who are vegetarians, this is not mandatory.

Samhain is also a time of new beginnings. It is the Celtic New Year celebration and it carries with it many of the traditions more commonly associated with the Julian calendar's New Year's Eve on December 31. Samhain is a time to put behind us those things we know are baneful. It is a time of change, a time for new beginnings. Magickally, it is the perfect time to quit smoking or end other habits which are harmful to mind or body. Oftentimes a besom is used to ritually sweep the home of the previous year's influence.

Masks are often made either to introduce new attributes or cast off old habits. If you want to quit smoking, don a mask of yourself as a smoker while in circle. Before you leave circle, cast the mask into a fire and destroy it. Bury a pack of cigarettes in a mini coffin. If you want to bring in new attributes, enter circle with no mask but leave with a mask that symbolizes the attributes you wish to acquire in the coming year.

Because Samhain is both the death of the old year and the birth of the new year, it is said that the veil between the worlds of the living and the dead is the thinnest on this day. Thus makes it a time to remember our ancestors. Altars are frequently decorated with photographs of loved ones who have passed into the next world, while their favorite foods and beverages are served to guests. Samhain is also a good time to ask those who have left this world for advice. Divination with the assistance of those who have crossed to the next world is especially effective in conjunction with the celebration of this holiday. Just keep in mind that if Uncle Harold crossed ten years ago, he probably won't be the best advisor on the current stock market.

Ritual Ideas

The Samhain ritual is very participatory. Everyone in attendance is welcome to bring pictures of loved ones who have crossed into the next world and guests are invited to bring their loved one's favorite dish, if food will be involved.

Traditionally, the altar is decorated with the colors of the season. This is one of the only times a black altar cloth is appropriate. Our culture associates black with endings. That is exactly what Samhain is. Of course with all endings, a beginning emerges. Orange is also appropriate as orange is the color of many of the last vegetables to be harvested. Gourds are very welcome decorations. Many traditions replace quarter candles with jack o'lanterns during this rite.

If you have a large cauldron or other container suitable for water, fill it for scrying. This is a preferred form of divination at Samhain. If the room is dimly lit and the water is illuminated with candlelight, visions will often come to those who gaze into the water's depth. I have found that floating candles can be particularly effective for large groups. If you do not have a large enough container, small black bowls can be used. Casting runes, reading tarot, and other forms of divination are most appropriate during the Samhain ritual.

Winter Solstice: A Quarter Day

ASSOCIATED GEMS: Bloodstone, garnet, and ruby
ASSOCIATED FOODS: Dried fruits and meats, sweets, and
   heavy foods
ASSOCIATED SPICES AND HERBS: Bay, ginger, and sage
ALSO KNOWN AS: Alban Arthan, Midwinter, Return of the
   Sun, Saturnalia, and Yule (It can also be associated with
   Mothers' Night and the Day of Children.)

The Winter Solstice is one of the most significant solar events of the year. Since the Summer Solstice the hours of daylight have been getting shorter and shorter. Winter Solstice is the shortest day of the year. From this point the days begin to grow longer, which is why this holiday is celebrated as the return of the sun. Night-long vigils are held, often with drumming and dancing, until dawn when the sunrise is greeted as if it were a long lost friend. Then the drumming intensifies and bells are added to ring in the return of the sun. The energy continues to build until the dancers and drummers are exhausted. Small fires replace bonfires for both symbolic and practical reasons. Symbolically, the smaller fires better reflect the state of the sun during Winter Solstice. The practical reasons is that this celebration usually takes place indoors.

When one considers the tremendous impact the sun has on our day-to-day lives, it is easy to understand why the ancients felt it appropriate to commemorate this solar event. Modern medicine has determined that lack of sunlight can contribute to depressive disorders such as Seasonal Affective Disorder (S.A.D.), thus confirming the ancients' observation that the Winter Solstice is a great time for a really good party.

More than any other, this sabbat is the easiest for recent initiates of Wicca to adjust to. This is because so much of the Christmas celebration has been taken directly from the practices of the ancient Pagans. Wreaths symbolize the turning wheel of the year. The green color is the promise of the return of vegetation in the spring. Bells are used to ring in the new sun. Even the predominant culture's "Christmas tree" was originally a Pagan tradition. In time of old, it was thought that by bringing the Yule tree indoors, the home would become more hospitable for nature spirits who were welcomed to the solstice rites. Today's Pagan often practice this custom by purchasing a living tree and bringing it into their home for Winter Solstice and the remainder of the winter. It is later planted outside.

The time between the Winter Solstice and the Summer Solstice is personified by the Oak King. The time between the Summer Solstice and the Winter Solstice on the opposite half of the Wheel is given the name Holly King. At the solstices, there is often ritualistic combat between two men and a symbolic victory. At Winter Solstice, the Oak King is the victor. (See below.)

Winter Solstice is also a time for family, children, and the home. Storytelling is appropriate, and not just for the children. Heavy foods are often served, often laced with sage to aid digestion.

Ritual Ideas

Use a yellow or gold altar cloth to symbolize and welcome the returning sun. Other appropriate colors to celebrate the season are red, green, and white.

The fight between the Holly King and the Oak King is a classic way to mark the Winter Solstice. If you can find both holly and oak leaves, create a crown of each. Volunteers are needed to play each king and wear the corresponding crown. Dull swords or staffs can be used and the battle should be previously choreographed. At the end of the battle, the Holly King falls to a blow from the Oak King.

Other ways to show the birth of the waxing sun and the death of the waning sun can include the passing of a torch from the Holly King to the Oak King, or a resurrection ritual may be performed. For the resurrection, the Holly King wears a crown of horns (symbolic of the horned God) and stands beside the Oak King, who lies on the ground shrouded in black cloth. The Holly King removes the black cloth from the Oak King and helps him to his feet. They embrace and the Holly King places the horned crown on the Oak King's head. The Holly King then lies down and the Oak King places the black cloth over him.

Another way to ritually celebrate the return of the sun while vanquishing darkness starts in almost total darkness. The Priestess and coven members raise the temple with the Priest noticeably missing. At the point where God is invited into the circle, the Priest appears outside the circle. He carries a candelabra with twelve yellow candles, one for each moon (month) of the year. Two coven members open the gate by lifting the broom and the Priest enters the circle. The symbolism is rarely missed when those in attendance understand what is being celebrated.

The tradition of creating a Yule log is alive and well. Decorate a log with greens and reds, using as much natural material as possible. If you have a fireplace, burn the log during the celebration. If you do not, mount three candlestick holders on the log. Instead of burning the log, light the candles. It is a good idea to spray the decorations with mist before lighting the candles so they don't catch fire. For the same reason do not allow the candles to burn down to the wood.

Cakes and cookies shaped like the sun are often shared during the Winter Solstice as a promise of the sun's return. If an Oak King has been chosen, he is the perfect choice to distribute the cakes and cookies. Some groups use a specific dish, also shaped like the sun, on which they serve these treats. The fire altar is often decorated with sun images and the main altar is draped in yellow.

It is also appropriate to celebrate through the night, greet the sunrise, and then hold ritual in the full light of the new sun. If alcohol will be a part of the festivities, hold the celebration after the rite. Meet early in the morning and time your rite so that it will end either at or just before the sunrise. Then the celebration can begin with less concern for overindulging.

Imbolg: A Cross-Quarter Day

ASSOCIATED GEMS: Amethyst and turquoise
ASSOCIATED FOODS: Milk, honey, and dried goods
ASSOCIATED SPICES AND HERBS: Rosemary and dill
ALSO KNOWN AS: Anagantios, Candlemas, Disting-tid, Feast
    of Brigid, Feast of the Virgin, Festival of Light, Festival of
    Milk, and Oimelc

Imbolg, also spelled Imbolc, which literally means "in belly," denotes the main focus of celebration at this time. This is the time of the year when Goddess, in her manifestation as Earth, feels the first stirrings of life in her womb and offers the promise of new life in the summer ahead. Although unseen, the first sprouts of seeds sown by nature have begun just below the surface of the earth at this time. As with all celebrations, the actual format of the rite will vary from group to group while the intent remains relatively similar: to stir the seed within the earth back into life.

On the wheel of the year, Imbolg falls halfway between the Winter Solstice and Spring Equinox. When the year was divided into the two seasons, this was the midpoint.

Ritual Ideas

At this celebration, the altar is decorated with a white cloth to symbolize the purity of the land. Yellow and pink decorations are also welcome. These colors closely resemble the color of sprouts before they reach sunlight. Although not entirely traditional, an appropriate food for this celebration is bean sprouts.

In both ancient and modern times, this holy day has been celebrated by the creation of a fertility scene. Men and women share the chore of preparing Brigid's bed. (This tradition has probably survived because the fertility Goddess

Bridid was adopted by the Catholic church as Saint Bridget.) The women create a doll and basket, both woven from the previous year's grain crop, to represent the Goddess Brigid and her bed. The men prepare an object to symbolize the God. This most often takes the form of a phallic-shaped wand. Once the men and women are finished, the wand (male symbol) and the doll (female symbol) are placed in Brigid's Bed (the basket) and the basket is taken from the circle to a place where the "lovers" can enjoy privacy.

I use the word lovers to refer to the contents of the basket for two reasons. The first is symbolic, as it is hoped that the act of putting these items together will help stir the earth's act of creating new growth and that the fertility represented symbolically in this rite will aid the fertility of the land. The second is because a couple who is hoping to conceive will be the ones chosen to take the basket to a place of privacy. It is said that on this night and in this way, the fertility of the land and of the couple can be shared and that each will conceive new life. If there are several couples who wish to conceive, a set can be made for each couple.

Back in circle, singing, chanting, and drumming, along with other merriment, should continue as the couple makes love. When the couple feels the spark of life has entered Brigid, they should return in modest fashion and announce that the spark of life has entered the earth. The actual wording should be from the heart and can come from different couples at different times, should several couples take part.

If there is not a couple that desires conception present, a couple in the group should still be appointed to bring the bed to a private spot, except instead of consummating the return of the seed to the earth, they should meditate and visualize the conception. When they concur that life has returned to the earth, the couple should return to the circle in like fashion and make a similar announcement. I strongly

suggest that lovers who do not wish to conceive on this
night refrain from consummating the evening, even with
modern birth control measures

Spring Equinox: A Quarter Day

ASSOCIATED GEMS: Aquamarine, moonstone, and rose quartz
ASSOCIATED FOODS: Eggs, honey, sweetbreads, and ginger candy
ASSOCIATED SPICES AND HERBS: Ginger
ALSO KNOWN AS: Alban Eilir, Bacchanalia, Eostre's Day,
     Lady Day, and Ostara

Although celebrations of the equinoxes do not have as long
a history as those of the solstices, they are definitely a clear
part of modern Wiccan celebrations. More than anything
else, the equinoxes are a time of balance, not only between
day and night, but between all forces in opposition. The
Spring Equinox is sometimes called the "waxing equinox"
because although the day and night are in balance on this
day, the length of the day is growing.

Few can look outside and not see the changes in the land.
Because the seasonal changes are so evident, modern culture
has adopted many of the ancient traditions. Four leaf
clovers, spring flowers, and even Easter eggs were originally
associated with Pagan traditions at this time of the year.

The celebration of the Spring Equinox centers around the
fertility of the land. The first flowers of spring are given as
gifts and often used to decorate the home. The signs of
what will hopefully be a fruitful year have broken ground.
Hardier plants are already flowering and awaiting pollen.

Ritual Ideas

Decorate the altar with green and yellow fabrics. The green
is for the vegetative earth which has begun to show itself,

while the yellow represents the sun that is at balance. Use spring flowers to adorn all the altars, particularly pink, red, yellow, and blue ones.

What are now commonly called Easter eggs were originally Pagan symbols of fertility, so hard-boiled eggs are more than welcome on the Spring Equinox altar. Decorate them with the colors of the season and exchange and eat them during your ritual. Although the day and night are equal at this point, the sun is waxing, making this a solar celebration. With its yellow yoke, what could make a better symbol of both the new birth of spring and of the sun itself? Decorating eggs also provides a wonderfully interactive activity.

Ritually filling a flower pot with potting soil, a handful from each in attendance, and then placing seeds into the soil is wonderfully symbolic gesture. Having everyone water it is nice too. If you like this idea, why not have enough flower pots and seeds for everyone? That way they can take what they have planted as a reminder of the kinship they have shared.

Bealtaine: A Cross-Quarter Day

ASSOCIATED GEMS: Bloodstone and sapphire
ASSOCIATED FOODS: Cheese and dairy, honey, sweets, and rose candy
ASSOCIATED SPICES AND HERBS: Rose petals and rosemary
ALSO KNOWN AS: Beltane, Cyntefyn, May Eve, Roodmass, and Walpurgis

The exact date of Bealtaine is halfway between Spring Equinox and Summer Solstice. Opposite Samhain, Bealtaine is one of the two most important high holy days. Before the year was split into four seasons, these dates marked the beginning of winter and summer, respectively.

Bealtaine is first and foremost a fertility festival. Unlike Spring Equinox, the primary focus at Bealtaine is human sexuality and fertility. Crop fertility is still a part of the celebration, but it is less of a priority. Still, when you live off the land every little bit helps. In the ancient rituals, couples were sent to the fields to make love. It was believed that having sex in the fields would encourage crop fertility. Today, when most Pagans do not live directly off the land, fertility can be shared in other areas. It is widely believed that this is why the ritual tools created in the workshops in the Legion Art Guild are popular in the Pagan community.

More symbolic gestures can be found surviving in today's culture. The maypole is such a blatant phallic symbol that it was outlawed in England between 1648 and 1660 C.E. (the Commonwealth period). Dancing around the maypole is a perfect example of the veneration of the male, which has often been obscured from the modern Witchcraft movement in the United States.

The hunting for nuts, possibly a predecessor to the Easter egg hunt, is another example of how the male forces were honored by the ancients. The nuts were symbolic testicles. The common Bealtaine practice of leaping the fire is also alive and well. Pregnant women would leap the fire to ensure a safe childbirth, maidens would leap the flames for future fertility, and other women would perform this act for general blessings. When one takes into consideration that gender association with the element fire is male, we might see thousands of natural phallic symbols in the flames. When I was in Germany, I found that the tradition of lighting "Bel-fires" atop hills and mountains is still observed. I have been told this is still a common practice throughout Europe. It is certainly alive and well in modern Wiccan rites.

Although human fertility takes precedence at Bealtaine, it is also the beginning of the growing season. The first signs of successful planting are starting to poke through the ground. Speculators can see a good harvest in its infancy.

Bealtaine also presents another celebration where drummers and dancers customarily celebrate throughout the night and into the next morning. This time they do so not to mark the return of the sun, but to set the beat and mood for love. Lovers dance and sing in between multiple visits to the fields or other appropriate locations. The next day the ashes of the ritual fire are spread between crops and carried in sachets for fertility of all types.

Ritual Ideas

If you really must celebrate inside, drape everything you can with green and use reds and yellows to spice things up. However, it is far better to celebrate outside where the earth has done the decorating for you. Bealtaine is one of the celebrations that should really be conducted outside around a huge bel-fire. Let the grass and vegetation provide the greens and the fire will give the reds and yellows.

In their book *Eight Sabbats for Witches*, Janet and Stewart Farrar suggest a lovers' chase at the Bealtaine ritual. After the circle is cast, the Priest takes a green scarf and tries to capture the Priestess with it. Once she relents and allows him to capture her, he hands the scarf to another male member who pushes his mate into the circle and tries to catch her. The chase continues in this manner until everyone who wants a turn has had a turn and the scarf is returned to the Priest. If someone in attendance is not with partner, it is very appropriate for the Priest or Priestess to either play matchmaker or act as a surrogate for the purpose of the game. This is a wonderfully appropriate way of stirring the hearts towards love and can be viewed as the chase between Pan and the nymphs.

The symbolic Great Rite sometimes takes place with the Priestess lying on the altar (or other appropriate surface) with the chalice held in her hands above the womb. The Priest stands at her side and lowers the athame into the chalice. More expressive groups might have the Priestess lie with her legs spread and bent at the knee over the edge of the altar. She holds the chalice in the same manner but the Priest stands between her knees as he lowers the athame. Neither of these suggestive gestures is necessary, but each seems especially appropriate at Bealtaine.

Summer Solstice: A Quarter Day

ASSOCIATED GEMS: Emerald, jade, lapis, and tiger's eye
ASSOCIATED FOODS: Lemon, orange, and other citrus, and
   early squash
ASSOCIATED SPICES AND HERBS: Lemon peel, melissa, and saffron
ALSO KNOWN AS: Alban Hefin, Litha, Midsummer, Vestalia,
   Whitsuntide, and sometimes Beltane

Summer Solstice is the longest day of the year and the height of male and solar energy. It is a time of great fertility in the land. Women who wish to conceive should walk among the crops in the hopes of acquiring fertility. This is perhaps the most festive holiday of the year. With the sun at its peak and the land at its ripest, life becomes easier and there is much to be grateful for.

Like Winter Solstice, this is a good time to serve cakes and cookies shaped like the sun. However, at Summer Solstice this is more of a feast than a promise. The sun is now at its fullest. Cheese is often served along with round loafs of golden bread (whole-grain bread is the best). If a Holly King has been chosen, he is the perfect choice to distribute the cakes and cookies. If you still have the dish used at Winter Solstice, it is most appropriate to reuse it at the Summer Solstice. Remember that the Holly King and Oak King are but different aspects of the same sun.

The main altar is often draped in yellow, symbolic of the sun. Sunflowers are a perfect way to decorate the altar as are all yellow and red flowers. Sunflower seeds are often scattered and shared. Gold is the preferred jewelry for this sabbat. Metals like brass, bronze, and even copper are also very welcome.

Ritual Ideas

Colors for Summer Solstice include yellow and gold for the sun as well as greens for the lush state of the earth. This is a good time to decorate the altar with sun symbols and to burn gold candles.

At Summer Solstice, the sun changes from waxing to waning. Like the conflict at Winter Solstice, this solstice has also been represented with the idea of conflict between the Oak King (waxing) and the Holly King (waning). But at Summer Solstice, the Oak King falls to the Holly King. This battle is re-created symbolically with sacred plays.

Although this is the longest day of the year, the sun has reached its peak and will begin to wane. Ritually extinguishing candles and lessening fires are often worked into this rite.

Lughnasadh: A Cross-Quarter Day

ASSOCIATED GEMS: Citrine and peridot

ASSOCIATED FOODS: Grain and potato breads and first harvest items

ASSOCIATED SPICES AND HERBS: Rye and ginseng

ALSO KNOWN AS: Ceresalia, Elembiuos, First Harvest, Lad Day, and Lammas

Lugnasadh takes its name from Lugh, an Irish God form.
At times, Lugh was known as Lugh Samhioldanach, Lugh
of the Many Arts. He was also called Lugh Lamhfhada,
Lugh of the Long Hand. I am undecided on whether the
long hand was another reference to his talent with the arts
or perhaps a pleasant way of describing another part of his
anatomy. I am particularly fond of him with either meaning. In fact, he is the patron deity of my studio/workshop.

On the Wheel of the Year, Lughnasadh falls halfway
between Summer Solstice and Autumn Equinox. The central theme at Lughnasadh is abundance. This is the first
harvest of the year. As such, food should always be part of
the celebration. Corn and other grains are excellent choices
in American culture as they come directly from our own
land. This is another ritual that is best celebrated outdoors.

Ritual Ideas

The Lughnasadh altar is appropriately decorated with red,
yellow, green, orange, and other harvest themes. Instead of
using one altar cloth, try several of different colors to signify the variety and plenty of the harvest.

Becasue this is a harvest celebration, the ritual should
reflect thanking the God and Goddess for what the first
harvest has brought. One of the nicest ways I have found
to accomplish this is to scatter breads, cookies, and other
baked goods outside your circle or into a wood line. Before
consuming any food, take out a portion and set it aside as
an offering. After the circle is broken, scatter the food
where you will. This is particularly symbolic if you are a
city dweller who is celebrating this holiday in natural sur-
roundings. In addition to thanking the earth for her bounty,
you are thanking the creatures who have allowed you to
use their home for your rite.

To associate your rite with both the harvest and with Lugh, try finding ways to use the nonedible portions of the harvest for craft materials. Dolls can be woven from the remnants of corn, wheat, and many other grains. Corn silk is excellent for doll hair. Dolls make wonderful gifts for children and can even be set aside for later use in spellcraft. Similar materials can be woven into mats, rough fabrics, and other goods. Scarecrows or big dolls can be made and placed in the fields to guard the next two harvests. If you have saved gourds from last years' Autumn Equinox, this is the perfect time to fashion them into rattles for the next Autumn Equinox.

The ritual breaking of bread is very welcome at Lughnasadh. Round breads can be cut into eighths to symbolize the eight-spoked Wheel of the Year. Serve it moving clockwise, symbolizing the turning of the year.

In their book *Eight Sabbats for Witches*, Janet and Stewart Farrar also suggest conducting a lovers' chase, such as the one at the Bealtaine ritual. Connecting this celebration with human sexuality might support the latter association of Lugh of the Long Hand.

Autumn Equinox: A Quarter Day

ASSOCIATED GEMS: Amethyst and topaz
ASSOCIATED FOODS: Apples, grapes, and nuts
ASSOCIATED SPICES AND HERBS: Hops and hazelnuts
ALSO KNOWN AS: Alban Elfed, Mabon, Festival of Dionysus, Second Harvest, and Wine Harvest

The Autumn Equinox is the second harvest. Again, the central theme is abundance, but with the balance of the Equinox and the knowledge that there is only one harvest left before winter. Feasting is welcome, but excessive indulgence is ill advised. The paradox is that this is also the time of the wild hunt of Dionysus (Greek) when overindulgence is thought to be the standard.

Some traditions hold that the time after gathering the second harvest is a time of rest and reflection, a time to begin planning the next year's planting. Because the second harvest is the grain harvest, much of what was taken in must be set aside for next year's growth. By this time it will be clear just how plentiful the winter food supply will be. Either the season has been prosperous and there will be enough food to feed both the village and the cattle, or the winter will be hard. But even when the worst is realized, this is a harvest time so the spirit is celebration.

Another way of thinking is that two of the three harvests are complete and the work year has peaked. It's time to celebrate not only in the harvest but in the fact that the work year is downhill from here. Dionysus and his Roman correlate Bacchus fit this role to the letter. As God of wine, he was worshiped with ecstatic and often orgiastic rituals which might rival those of Bealtaine.

One might declare the middle road between contemplative reflection and ecstatic ritual might be the wisest choice. After all, equinox is a time of balance.

Ritual Ideas

The Autumn Equinox altar is most often draped in brown and orange cloth. Leaves and gourds are appropriate if they are readily available in your area. Horns of plenty are most appropriate, especially when their contents are consumed during the rite.

Drumming and dancing are very welcome, as they are on each of the Sabbats, but the Autumn Equinox festivities cry out for gourd rattles. Put a few gourds from this year's harvest aside to be dried and made into rattles for next year's celebration.

If you serve a food that will keep for three months, ritually place it aside and serve it at Winter Solstice. It is also a good time to start food drives for local shelters. Food collected prior to this event can be ritually blessed during the rite and then given to shelters on the following day.

Fusing Ancient Lore Into Modern Celebrations

I have seen dozens of books which spell out specific rituals for each of the sabbats. At the end of this book, you will find much of Creation's Covenant's current book of rituals, or Book of Shadows. In that collection, none of the rites are overly formal or somber. It is my belief that somber or formal rites could never belong to Pagans. We common folk don't seem very attracted to formalities.

You can find references to the sabbats in at least half of the books on Witchcraft. Many of these are good examples of what has worked for others, but what is important is what works for you. While these celebrations are related to the natural cycles of the earth, they key in on your relationship with the earth. Only you can fill in that blank and create a meaningful ritual.

9

Moons and Suns as Times of Power

The Moon and Lunar Cycles

It seems that although inanimate objects can be given gender and not sex, once we personify a symbol, it receives sex. For the purposes of this book, sex is the combination of both the male and the female gender, with one of the two in dominance. Just as each human is made up of both genders, each symbol we personify is both male and female.

With an understanding of the difference between gender and sex, we can say that the moon personified is female because both historically and today it appears to be a combination of both the male and female gender, though it is predominantly expressed as female. (See the charts on pages 28 and 36 for Moon Goddesses and Moon Gods, respectively.) This makes the moon a symbol that can be personal to men as well as women. Her powers need not be foreign to the male psyche any more than our own attributes, both male and female, do.

Female-Gendered Energy
and the Lunar Cycles

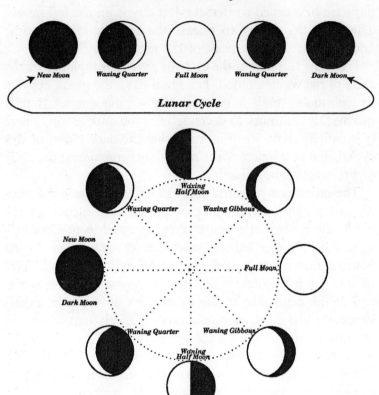

To know the moon, we must understand her cycles. There are approximately twenty-eight days of each lunar cycle. The discrepancy is due to the fact that our system of measuring time is based on both the lunar (months and weeks) and solar (years and days) calendar. The moon cycle begins with the new moon (first quarter), grows over seven days into the waxing quarter (second quarter), then continues to grow for another seven days into the full moon (third quarter). During this two-week period, lunar energies are building. I have found that spells which take several days are best timed so that the last day is on the full moon. This way, the energy to release the spell builds over time and is released at the peak of the moon's power.

From the full moon, the cycle of growth is replaced by the cycle of the waning moon. For seven days, the moon appears to get smaller until it becomes the waning quarter (fourth quarter). It continues to decrease until the dark moon, where it is entirely dark. Keep in mind that the dark moon of this cycle is the new moon of the next, thus perpetuating the cycle of life, death, and rebirth

The moon is a powerful force in nature Because the tides give us a constant reminder of the moon's impact on the earth, the moon's effects are often accepted in modern culture. Ask a police officer, bartender, or cab driver during which moon phase it is the worst to work. You will likely be told the full moon. When the full moon falls on a weekend at the beginning of the month, it's even worse. Emergency rooms, bars, morgues, and jails all experience an increase in business. Even the words "lunacy" and "lunatic" have their roots in lunar events. In common lore, the full moon has been the time when afflicted men and women turn into werewolves, when men and women are driven insane, and when lovers are drawn together.

Definitions, Timing, and Powers
of the Monthly Lunar Cycles

Many covens and solitary practitioners convene on the nights of the lunar cycles. These meetings are called esbats. They most often commemorate the full moon, sometimes the new moon, and occasionally, the quarter moons. Unlike the sabbats, which are mainly for celebration alone, the esbats are generally used for the workings of magick and spellcraft. They are often much shorter than the sabbat celebrations and should always be conducted on the actual night of the lunar event for the best results.

The new moon is associated with the beginning of the Maiden stage of the Triple Goddess, and is a good time for dedications and blessings of children as well as a time of new beginnings. Love spells to start new relationships are especially effective during the new moon. Covens and solitary practitioners who honor the new moon as an esbat often conduct initiations with this theme. The waxing quarter is also associated with the Maiden stage of the Triple Goddess. Now is a good time for spellcraft that involves growth or building the structures of life. The Maiden lends her hand during this time to spells designed to generate increased lust.

The full moon is strongly associated with the Mother stage of the Triple Goddess. It is a good time for fertility and prosperity spells. A marriage that is consummated under the full moon is said be both fruitful and prosperous. Covens and solitary practitioners who do not hold esbats at the new moon often initiate at the full moon as it is a time of conception.

The waning quarter is associated with the beginning of the Crone stage of the Triple Goddess. It is a time when Mother energy fades into Crone energy and when spells to bind and decrease one's energy are particularly effective. Conduct a binding spell on the waning quarter and watch the bound person's negative aspects fade over seven days until they wink out at the dark moon.

The dark moon is also strongly associated with the Crone stage of the Triple Goddess and is a good time to confront the loss of a loved one, to honor ancestors, and

to communicate with other realms. Because the Crone is
the Grandmother, this is also an excellent time to ask for
divine intervention and protection of pregnant women,
especially in the latter part of pregnancy. Don't forget that
in the way that death and rebirth are parts of the same
process, so the dark moon and new moon are parts of
each other.

There are most often twelve and sometimes thirteen
moon cycles each year. Each has a specific name and
associated aspects. Use an astrological calendar to determine the full lunar cycle, from new moon waxing into the
full moon and then waning into dark moon. Determine
which month contains the majority of that moon and look
up that month on the following chart.

Names and Associations to Lunar Events

Month	Primary Moon Name	Saxon Moon Name	Alternative* Moon Name	Primary Color	Primary Gem(s)
January	Wolf Moon	Wulf-Monat	Ice Moon	White	Garnet
February	Storm Moon	Mire-Monat	Wild Moon	Red	Amethyst
March	Chastle Moon	Hraed-Monet	Storm Moon*	Green	Aquamarine, Bloodstone
April	Seed Moon	Eastre-Monat	Planters' Moon	Brown	Diamond
May	Hare Moon	Preo-meolc-Monat	Frogs Moon	Pink	Emerald
June	Partner Moon	Saer-Monat	Mead Moon*	Purple	Moonstone, Pearl
July	Mead Moon	Maed-Monat	Harvest Moon*	Green	Ruby
August	Wort Moon	Wyrt-Monat	Barley Moon*	Yellow	Peridot, Sardonyx
September	Barley Moon	Gust-Monat	Harvest Moon*	Brown	Sapphire
October	Blood Moon	Wyne-Monat	Hunters' Moon	Blue	Opal
November	Snow Moon	Blot-Monat	White Moon	Green	Topaz
December	Oak Moon	Yule-Monat	Long Moon	Red	Turquoise

* Other names can be found throughout the world's diverse cultures. The
Chastle Moon is sometimes spelled Chaste. Some names are used more than
once depending on the culture and seasonal differences around the world. This
is particularly true with the term "harvest moon." Names, colors, and gems
listed as "primary" are the most common correspondences in Creation's
Covenant.

The Wolf Moon is the first full lunar cycle after the Winter Solstice. It is a time when the new year of the modern calendar has begun. In magick, it is an excellent time to plan new goals and directions, preferably from the comfort of a warm den. Love magick is particularly effective during this moon if your intent is to bring a new love into your life. This is also the case for money. This moon is an excellent time for spellcraft aimed at acquiring a new job or promotion. Works of healing for the joints and skin seem popular during this month, though this is probably out of necessity rather than increased effectiveness.

In February, the Storm Moon presents an excellent time for purification and tempering rites and a time to affirm and strengthen resolutions made during the Wolf Moon. If you have a loved one who has done you wrong, this is a good time to rid yourself of the anger you might still harbor. Spellcraft aimed at helping the elderly or improving the quality of living experienced by those who are terminally ill is best performed at this time.

The Chastle Moon is a time of innocence and the preferred month for Wiccanings—the dedication of young children to the Wiccan path. Money and prosperity spells are very effective now. Chastle Moon is a time to ask the Lord and Lady to smile on new crops, endeavors, and ventures.

When full, the extra light of the Seed Moon extends the work day. Farmers can work later into the night, planting the seeds to sow the year's abundance. It is also a time when new projects, jobs, and endeavors should receive extra attention. If you begin something new during this moon, you will see an improved return at harvest time. Spellcraft to improve a sexual relationship and for conception of a child is particularly effective during this moon. Some say that it is unlikely that a healthy couple who makes love under the full Seed Moon will not conceive. Even with modern birth control, if you do not want to conceive a child it is best to abstain from sex during this moon.

The Hare Moon is the second best moon for fertility and conception spellcraft. It is also a time of rebirth, especially of the land. Lore tells us that this is the absolute worst moon to form marriages and other partnerships. However, it is an excellent time to consider the possible pending commitments of either. Men should think about asking their lovers for commitment now, but make the decision and ask during the next moon

Planning on formalizing a relationship? The Partner Moon is, as the name implies, an excellent moon during which to marry or to propose It is also a good time to forge new business relations, to improve family relations, and to bond with friends. Spellcraft aimed at these goals, as well as strengthening, cleansing, love, and protection, is particularly suited for this moon. It is said that if you can cheat on a lover or business partner during this moon that your heart is truly cold. Partners of all types takes note; you may forgive one who is unfaithful during this moon but it is best not to forget, not yet.

The Mead Moon is a time of celebration and of being thankful. It is a good time to give what you can to charities. Karma will reward you later. Spilling mead or wine on the ground shows the earth your appreciation for all that you have harvested that year. Spellcraft aimed at love, health, money, and any other nurturing and building goals is especially effective during this moon.

The Wort Moon is sometimes called the Plant Moon because wort literally means "plant." This moon takes its name from the fullness of plant life during its reign. The

Wort Moon can be seen as a woman who is nine months pregnant, about to burst forth with life. It is a time to be bold, like the lion, in our decisions, as well as for concentration and meditation before we make those decisions. The Wort Moon is a good time for spells that focus on wisdom and logic. Listen to your dreams and trust your intuition with temperament during this moon.

The Barley Moon is a good time to revel in a job well done. If your business has been prosperous, a few extra dollars in key employees' checks will be rewarded by their continued loyalty. Offerings from your harvest are accepted particularly well during this moon. Courting and spells aimed at making you more attractive to a potential mate as well as spells to ensure good health through the winter are appropriate at this time.

Taking its name from the necessary hunting and slaughter of animals at the onset of Winter, the Blood Moon signaled the need to begin hunting for winter. In areas where animals were raised for milk, eggs, and their skins, this was the time when the grain harvest was measured and portioned for the pending winter. If there was not enough food to feed the animals throughout the winter, surplus animals were put to death and used for food rather than allowing them to starve. The Blood Moon is a time of somber decisions. Spellcraft for protection, reversal, and justice is particularly effective and rituals to thank ancestors are most appropriate at this time.

The Snow Moon is the promise of spring and of love. It is an excellent time to consult oracles and ancestors. Spellcraft against overindulgence, alcoholism, and chemical abuse is wonderfully effective during this moon. If there was an incident that you forgave but did not forget during the Partner Moon, this is a good time to forget. If you've made it this far, you should put the matter out of your mind for good.

During the Oak Moon, strength, vigilance, and endurance are most needed. This is when the sun is at its shortest cycle and depression fights to enter the psyche as forcefully as the cold fights to enter the body. Spellcraft to fight depression is a good idea as is purification of the mind, body, and soul. The Oak Moon is a good time to renew old partnerships and commitments, but it is a horrible time to make destructive decisions concerning interpersonal relationships, especially those concerning lovers. If you are having problems in a loving relationship, take only positive actions. Never consider ending a partnership during this moon. If there are problems, set them aside until the wolf moon or you may regret your decision.

The Blue Moon does not appear on the preceding chart because it is not an annual occurrence. The expression "once in a blue moon" is often used to convey a sense of rarity possibly because the Blue Moon can be seen only once every two and a half years. It is the product of our attempt to align both the solar and lunar cycles into a single calendar. The Blue Moon is the lunar cycle whose midpoint is the second full moon in any given month. It will most often take place in a month with thirty-one days (it will rarely be seen in April, June, September, or November) and will never occur in February.

A time of giving, the Blue Moon is the gift of time—an extra full moon under which to work. If the year has been prosperous thus far, this is a good time to give something extra to charity or to buy a gift for a loved one. If the year has not been prosperous, work late into the evening to catch up on things that might be holding back your potential during this moon.

The Suns and Solar Cycles

Like the moon, the sun is also said to possess both the male and female gender, but because historically and in modern times it has been seen to be predominantly male, we can say that its sex is male. See the charts on pages 27 and 34 for Sun Goddesses and Sun Gods, respectively.

In modern Wicca, solar celebrations are honored with the four cross-quarter sabbats. Unfortunately, the solar cycles are rarely consulted for the purpose of spellcraft and the working of male energy. During the persecution of the older religions, many took to the night to avoid detection. Bright colors and daytime celebrations stopped. It was easier to escape into the night in a robe of black than to hide in the daytime in a bright yellow robe. Even today, when religious freedom is better tolerated this trend continues. To make use of solar energy is to reclaim the day, to stop cowering in the shadows of night. Using these energies is also a way of reclaiming the male forces in our religion, to stand equal to our Goddess rather than cowering in her moonlight.

Solar energies are best used during the day. Although these solar events occur at the same time as four of the sabbats, it is better not to use these solar tides for magick and spellcraft in conjunction with the sabbat celebration, but before or after.

To know the sun we must understand his cycles. The most obvious is day and night. Even though the moon is most often associated with night, the sun and male energies can be linked to the night in the same way we link the dark moon to the sun's attributes. When we categorize the day this way, male energies can be assigned to day and night in the following wide generalizations:

Daytime is associated with cognitive functions and with the right side of the brain. Daylight hours are excellent for spellcraft aimed at improving business and resolving mental conflicts. Spells aimed at relationship matters other than love and passion are excellent if spun during the day.

Nighttime is associated with the intuitive functions, emotions, and with the left side of the brain. It is the best time for divination, fertility, healing, and especially primal and instinctive matters. Love spells are best if spun at night.

Additional general associations can be drawn with sunrise and sunset. Sunrise is a good time for new beginnings. It can lend a hand to bringing a new love into your life, blessing a new business, or starting a new Craft, among others. Sunset aids spellcraft aimed at endings and dwindling of energies. Bindings are particularly effective at sunset. Spells spun to lessen heartache are excellent now, especially when the following night and morning will be used for love magick.

The primary solar-cycle is commonly known as a year. At approximately 365 days, using its cycle will take some planning. The beginning of this cycle and mark of the first solar quarter is the Winter Solstice, the shortest day of the year. From this point on, the sun and length of the day grows into the second-quarter marker, the Spring Equinox. On this day, the length of night and day are equal. The length of the day continues to grow until the third quarter marker, the Summer Solstice, the longest day of the year. From this point, the sun and the length of the day becomes shorter. After approximately ninety-one days, the nights and days are once again equal at the fourth-quarter marker, the Autumn Equinox. The length of the day and effects of the sun continue to decrease until the rebirth of the cycle at Winter Solstice. While this explanation of the solar cycle might seem elementary to some, it seems that fewer and fewer people realize that the year is based on this solar cycle, with the solar quarters denoting the seasons.

Annual Solar Cycles and Associations*

Quarter Name	From	Approx. Date*	Until	Approx. Date*	Primary Color	Primary Gemstone
Winter	Winter Solstice	Dec. 20	Spring Equinox	Mar. 19	Green	Turquoise
Spring	Spring Equinox	Mar. 20	Summer Solstice	June 19	Yellow	Bloodstone
Summer	Summer Solstice	June 20	Autumn Equinox	Sept. 19	Red	Moonstone
Autumn	Autumn Equinox	Sept. 20	Winter Solstice	Dec. 19	Blue	Sapphire

*These dates are approximate. The exact date and specific time of the solstices and equinoxes are given in most astrological calendars. Failing that, you can usually find the information in the weather section of your local newspaper.

Male-Gendered Energy and the Seasons

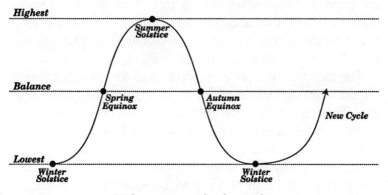

Male energy and solar cycles

At the beginning of the winter quarter, male-gendered energy is at its lowest but will wax throughout the quarter, so this is a good time to consider new relationships and partnerships. It is best to only carefully consider business ventures during this quarter and not act on them. Avoid making serious decisions during this quarter, especially in December, as December often makes or breaks relationships, partnerships, and businesses. Spellcraft aimed at justice, understanding, and clarity is especially effective during this cycle. Look to the moon and your feminine characteristics for strength, especially in accordance with the lunar cycles. Spellcraft drawing on the moon and female energies for strength, protection, and stability is a good idea.

Male-gendered energy is in balance at the beginning of the spring quarter, but will wax throughout, so this is a good time to commit to new relationships and partnerships, which you only considered during the last quarter. Business ventures have an extra blessing when started in the spring. This is a good time to make decisions, especially in March, as balance provides clarity. Spellcraft aimed at cleansing, new love, income, fertility, happiness, luck, and creativity are particularly effective during this cycle as well as spellcraft for abundance and prosperity for the future. Remember that the central theme of this quarter is planting the seeds of current goals for future fruition.

The summer quarter is a good time to revel in existing relationships and partnerships as male gendered energy is at its highest but will wane throughout the quarter. Business ventures often begin to demonstrate just how wise the decisions made last winter were. If they are showing signs of failure, this is the time when you should put forth that extra effort. It is also a good time to consider decisions wisely, especially in June. With the peak of male-gendered energy, we sometimes think we can conquer the world, but then fail miserably due to overly high expectations. Then again, sometimes we win. Spellcraft aimed at birth, energy, fruition, creativity, invention, productivity, and enhancing established relationships is especially effective during this quarter. The beginning of this cycle is of particular note to men as it is the point when male-gendered energy is most abundant.

At the beginning of the autumn quarter, male-gendered energy is in balance but will wane throughout so it is a good time to affirm existing relationships and partnerships. As in the summer quarter, in the autumn quarter, business ventures will demonstrate just how wise the decisions made last winter were. Spellcraft aimed at strengthening the family and home is timed very appropriately when conducted during this quarter. Affirmations of commitments made in the past year are a good idea. Divination and the consultation of ancestors are particularly effective and appropriate.

Sun and Moon in Balance

The Goddess Ataentsic (Iroquois and Huron) was said to have given birth to both the sun and moon. In fact, many deity forms were associated with both. Bhauani was a Hindu Goddess with the sun and moon as her breasts. Jara (Semetic) was originally a new moon God, but was later transformed by culture into the current feminine form. Kame and Keri (Caribbean) were twin brothers who gave the sun and moon specific paths.

As Wicca gives honor to the life force through the union of male and female, it seems natural that once the sun and moon have been personified, we would look to their union or synchronicity as times of great energy and creation. An obvious point of their union is the solar eclipse. Children that were conceived during a solar eclipse are said to be born with great potential. This is a good time for spellcraft aimed at union, love, and harmony between men and women, and a great time to hire a babysitter and get away from the kids so that parents can strengthen their ties to each other.

A time of solar and lunar separation can be seen in the lunar eclipse when the moon is eclipsed by the shadow of the earth. The lunar eclipse is a good time for spellcraft aimed at improving your relationship with children, particularly your own. Address issues that come between you and your lover. Other patterns of male and female energy being united by the sun and moon can also be found. Four of these are:

New moon at Winter Solstice	New beginnings
Waxing quarter moon at Spring Equinox	Growth and maturation
Full moon at Summer Solstice	Birth, fruition, and prosperity
Waning quarter moon at Autumn Equinox	Divination, endings, and new bindings

Each of these presents an excellent time to spin spells for relationships, union, love, and balance.

IO

Death and the Afterlife

There are ancient legends of people living for hundreds if not thousands of years, but there is very little documentation that validates such folklore. What we can document is that modern medicine has steadily provided longer lives. Researchers are making strides towards eliminating illness and better repairing injury. Politicians are forever attempting to stave off war and social threats. Loved ones pray for the recovery of the terminally ill. It seems that everyone wants to cheat death. But you can't. Death is a patient hostess. No matter how far we run, her hospitality awaits.

Historically, the moment of death has been defined as the last exhale. Many cultures believe the soul leaves the body with that final breath. Modern medicine defines death as the moment when brain activity stops (four or five minutes after the last breath). Each of these definitions falls short of my satisfaction. I choose to be the master of my own soul. I believe that the life force can leave the body at any time, either on command, as in astral travel, or upon death. I also believe the life force can refuse to leave for many years, perhaps explaining the existence of ghosts.

Souls that remain in this realm long after they have left their body are probably doing so for one of two reasons. In the case of sudden and unexpected death, it is likely that they don't feel they have reached a necessary level of completion to move on. Or they are afraid of what they will find if they do move on. With the many horrifying cultural images of death, it is easy to see why one might hesitate.

Today, death seems to take on two predominant personifications. Popular American culture most frequently views death as the Grim Reaper. Reaperlike characters have appeared as either skeletons or as repulsively emaciated. Contrary to the popular view that death is a masculine force, there are historical reaperlike images that were definitely female. Modgud (Teutonic), who guarded the bridge to the German concept of the underworld and had to be paid a token of blood to pass comes to mind. The other personification of death is a vision of beauty. The Angel of Death has been seen as the perfect lover, greeting us with open arms. There is historical precedence for each.

Although these two images seem entrenched in our modern culture, other images litter history. Like the Angel of Death, these personifications often took flight with the souls of the recently dead, but unlike the Angel of Death, many were other than human. Birds, particularly crows and vultures, seem popular. An old Tibetan death rite involved the dismembering of the deceased. The parts were then scattered for winged scavengers.

I have a nontypical view. I personify death as Grandmother and objectify her as the sleep that comes after an illness. She helps the ill through the sickness that is the end of life and tucks the sick into the bed that is death. In the morning, the next life, the sick wake healthy, refreshed from deep sleep and reincarnated in a new body.

Wiccan views on the afterlife are as diverse as those of any people. One of the most popular beliefs is in reincarnation. This is not an unusual belief. If you could tally up all the non-Western believers and add that number to the growing number of Westerners who follow this way of thinking, you would likely find that the majority of people believe in some form of reincarnation. It is not a new belief—historical records reveal that reincarnation was not only a tenet of early Christianity and Buddhism, but also that it is likely to be as old as language itself. Nor is it outdated. Past-life therapy, which could not exist without the concept of reincarnation, is now actively practiced.

Many Wiccans believe it is impossible, due to natural time limitations, to learn as much as is necessary in just one lifetime. Many look to the natural cycle of life to explain death—birth, life, death, and rebirth. Our bodies are born, we live, and we die. But upon closer examination, consider that when our bodies die, the natural course is to be returned to the earth. As our bodies decompose, they become nourishment for plants. Once in plant form, these nourishment's then find their way into women. When a woman is pregnant, her body builds a new life with the nourishment left behind by what is dead.

As Wiccans look to nature to find the patterns that others shrug off as supernatural, our concept of what happens to the soul after death is very similar to what takes place during the cycle of life. This belief can be called nonconscious reincarnation. It is the belief that our soul exists like a snowflake, completely different from any of its kind, but in time it melts and loses its individuality, blending with the water from other melting snowflakes. Eventually it evaporates and falls again as yet another totally unique individual.

In its second incarnation, it has parts of the first incarnation and parts of other incarnations, but the original individual is gone forever. This concept can be frightening to people at first. Many shy away from it and favor the more accepted belief that each soul is reincarnated intact. However, when one considers the true scope of infinite probability, it becomes less scary. You see, infinity is just a number that is larger than we can conceive of.

Because each snowflake comes from the very finite amount of water in our biosphere, there is a finite number of snowflakes, but it is larger than we can comprehend. The water to make each snowflake is constantly mixing with other water in each cycle, but it is mixing without the individual pattern of the snowflake intact. Although a new snowflake is made from a water mixture that has been many different snowflakes, only a finite number of snowflakes may occur. Because it is not possible to distinguish one water molecule from the next, the new snowflake pattern may be identical to the one before it even if it contains none of the matter from the first. With the pattern repeated, our consciousness does not die. When considering reincarnation, I doubt that anyone feels our new bodies are made from the same material as our former bodies. Why then do so many insist that the life force that is within the new body is the identical life force that was in our former body?

Those who subscribe to conscious reincarnation believe that at death our consciousness is transferred intact. Some teachings say that it is transferred directly into the body of the recently conceived, while others instruct that the soul joins the body at birth or at the first breath.

With either view of reincarnation, Wiccans often believe there is a place for the life energy between incarnations. This is most often called the Summer Land. Its name expresses the idealistic resting place of a people who worked the land for a living. Remember that when you live off the land as the Pagans of old did, "summer" can be appropriately translated as "with food." The Summer Land can be the place where cattle need not be slaughtered in the fall. It is a place where the harvest is plentiful and perpetual and where living is easy. I choose to believe Summer Land is here on earth. It is the earth as it may once have been, and the way it may be once again.

Most Wiccans do not believe in hell. I am not most Wiccans. History teaches that many of the original Pagans believed in a dark place, one where food and warmth was scarce. I choose to believe this place is also here on earth. It is the earth the way it might one day be. To escape this eventuality, we need only recognize its possibility. Call it what you will. Winter Land, Nuclear Winter, I choose to call it cause and effect.

II

Sample Spells

Contained in this chapter are spells that I have used with success. It is not necessary to conduct these from within a ritually constructed circle or temple, but it can't hurt. Some have been taken from other sources and then changed to suit my needs; others I have written myself. I invite you to do the same. Think of this as a collection of my recipes. Try them the way they are, then add your own choices of spice. Personalize them and have fun.

Simple Spells to Attract Money

It is widely believed that if you burn a green candle that has been anointed with patchouly oil, it will bring you wealth. The same is said about wearing patchouly oil or putting it on the money you carry in your wallet. I have also seen references to powdering the herb and keeping it with your money or carrying it in a green sachet.

To improve business, it has been suggested that you place a piece of malachite in each corner of your business place. Better yet, put each piece of malachite in a green sachet with patchouly leaves. Dab a few drops of oil on the bags on the first Thursday of each month.

I have found that Thursday is the best day of the week for me to buy a lottery ticket. I still lose more than I win, but I seem to lose less when the tickets are bought on this day. I have a friend that swears that she is lucky at Bingo when she buys a new lodestone Thursday afternoon, then plays at night. If she loses, she brings her stone back to the store and exchanges it the following Thursday afternoon. She insists that the stone must be defective. Aventurine is another stone that is said to aid gambling.

Simple Spells to Attract Love

I have found using magick for matters of the heart to be a very bad idea. We tend to get what we ask for and when it comes to love, too often we only *think* we know what we want, confusing our will with our whim. Once we get what we've asked for, we wind up stuck with it. Love magick is best reserved for the brave and the foolish.

Rose quartz is said to draw love. To attract a woman, place a piece of rose quartz in a bag filled with leaves from our old friend patchouly. Anoint this bag with patchouly oil every Friday and carry it with you. If you don't want the added benefit of attracting money with the patchouly, substitute rose petals and rose oil. When you find out how much true rose oil costs you'll want to go back to the patchouly.

A blatant amulet to attract love is a piece of rose quartz carved into the shape of a heart. It works best if you have sparked an interest in someone already. If she asks you about it, tell her it is a gift that you have been keeping for her and present it to her. Other pendants which seem to work effectively are images of couples in an embrace, the talisman of Venus (see your local magick shop), and red sachets filled with a mixture of patchouly and cinnamon.

Simple Spells to Promote Healing

Of all the gemstones I have worked with, hematite, jasper, and sodalite seem the most effective for general healing. They work well in green sachets which are also filled with rosemary, juniper berries, and camphor, and work best if you assemble them on a Monday—but if you get sick on Wednesday, don't wait. Do *not* use healing magick as a substitute for a doctor's care.

Burn a candle that represents the sick person. As the flame burns into the candle, visualize a white light of healing energy entering the person's body.

Simple Spells for Protection

Buy some small round mirrors, black ribbon, and glue at your local craft store. Cut the ribbon to the length from the top of a window that you would like to shield to the bottom of the window (about three feet). Glue the mirrors back to back with the ribbon in the center. Place three pairs of mirrors on each ribbon and hang them in your window. It is widely believed that negative energy will bounce off the mirrors or be absorbed in the black ribbon.

Black salt—available at most shops that carry supplies for spellcraft—sprinkled between you and bad neighbors is said to keep them from interfering. Throw in a few pieces of hematite to ground their negative energy.

If you are using a pentacle, hang it above your doorway between rituals. Better yet, make one especially to guard your home. The pentagram that is carved on the pentacle is said to be a very powerful protection symbol. However, it is important that you do not place this device outside the home since the symbol might not be fully understood. It might attract more negative attention than it will cast off negative energy.

Asafetida in a black sachet is said to be a very powerful talisman of protection. Unfortunately, it smells so bad it will likely ward off your best friend as well. Its smell has been known to induce vomiting.

More Complex Spells

The more forethought, planning, and effort you put into a task the better the results will be. Spellcraft is no different. Here are a few longer spells that I have had success with. Remember, visualization is often the key to any spell.

A Spell to Attract a New Woman Into Your Life

MATERIALS: 1 pink human image candle of the appropriate sex
1 red human image candle of the appropriate sex
1 glass or chalice of water
3 pinches of salt
1 red sachet
Love drawing oil or essential oil of patchouly

TOOLS: Candle scribing tools
Shallow bowl
Matches or a lighter

The pink candle should be selected to represent you and the red to represent the love that you wish to bring into your life. To have a specific person in mind would be manipulative. Still, it is possible to personalize the candles and attune them to the type of person you would like to attract. You can personalize the candle that represents you in many ways: decorate it with your birth stone(s), affix a lock of your hair, inscribe your name into its base, and anoint it with oils that correspond to your zodiac symbol. Be creative. Use these ideas and your own. Do whatever you can to convince yourself that the candle is you, and then anoint it with the patchouly oil.

If you don't mind a huge amount of chaos and turbulent relationships, simply anoint the red candle with the patchouly oil. This will attract indiscriminately. If you would like to bring a specific type of person, check astrology books and other sources for desirable correspondences. Look for the personality traits that you would like to find in the person you want to draw into your life, then attune the candle to the zodiac sign that seems to be what you are looking for using similar methods as the pink candle. Refer to the charts in the resources section of this book.

Arrange a table facing east. It is best if you are by a window or outdoors where you can see the sunrise. Put the female candle on the left side of the table and the male candle on the right. The salt goes on the right, the glass or chalice of water on the left. The patchouly oil, shallow bowl, and red sachet go in the center.

Spinning the Spell

This spell is best spun on Friday night during the second period of Venus (see page 49). Light the pink candle, saying: "This candle is (*your name*)." Light the red candle, saying: "This candle is the love that I draw."

As the candles burn, gradually move them closer to the bowl no more than an inch at a time. Take your time and concentrate. As you do, visualize your love moving towards you, you towards your love, and both towards the relationship, symbolized here as the bowl. Realize that your partner is not the only one to move. Once both candles have reached the center of the work space, place them together in the bowl so that the melting wax will fuse.

From the left side of the table, take the glass of water, affirming that it represents the female forces in nature. Pour enough water into the bowl so that the melting wax will not contact the bottom of the bowl. Do not add so much water that the candles float and topple. From the right side of the table, take the salt, affirming that it represents the male forces in nature. Salt the water in the bowl three times. Realize that this is the fusion of male and female.

As the candles melt, their wax will drip together. In some areas the red and pink will fuse into a single color; in others, they will embrace but remain separate. The wax may take on a specific shape in the water. Study the way the red and pink wax blends. Observe the patterns of wax in the water as they appear and then as more wax changes them. Look for patterns, symbols, anything that might offer a message.

When the candles have gone out on their own and you have observed all that you can in the wax patterns, anoint the cooled wax with the patchouly and place it in the sachet. Wait for the sun to rise and as it does, consider the new day to be the promise of a new love. Until your love enters your life consider every sunrise the promise of things to come. Carry the sachet with you. Consult it at least once a day. See how the patterns change with time. When your love enters your life, it is best that you cast the sachet into a fire and destroy it.

A Spell to Bind Against Harm
and Eliminate a Magickal Threat

MATERIALS: 1 poppet or human image candle (to make a poppet, you will need a piece of fabric in the color of the person's skin)

Various herbs appropriate to the person's zodiac sign

The person's favorite perfume, oil, or other scent

1 black candle

2 sections of twine, each three feet long

1 wood box in which the poppet or human image candle fits

1 handful of nettle

1 handful of thistle

TOOLS: Scissors

Needle and thread

Matches or a lighter

Hammer and nails (if available)

Shovel

You can use the easy method of substituting a human image candle for the poppet, but I have had much more luck using a poppet of my own design. Just draw out the approximate shape of a human on a piece of fabric which appropriately represents the person's skin color. Cut the fabric along the outline and make a second to match it. Then stitch the two pieces together but leave an opening to add herbs appropriate to the person's zodiac sign. If you can get a lock of his or her hair, affix it to the poppet's head. If he or she smokes, stitch a cigarette to the poppet's hand. If he or she is overly con-

cerned with money, slide a dollar bill into the opening.
If you have some of his or her birthstones, place them
inside as well. Once the poppet is filled, stitch it shut.
Scent the poppet with the person's favorite perfume, oil,
or other scent.

Spinning the Spell

This spell is best spun on Saturday just before sunset. Light
the black candle. With one section of twine, wrap the poppet tightly from toe to head. As you do, say: "I bind you
(*name of person*) from doing harm." Repeat this over and
over until the cord is completely wrapped around the poppet. Tie the cord and drip the black wax over the twine to
prevent it from unraveling.

Place the bound poppet in the wood box. Take the nettle in your left hand and the thistle in your right. Add
them to the box on top of the poppet, again saying: "I
bind you (*name of person*) from doing harm." Close the
box. If you can nail it shut, do so. Wrap the second length
of twine around the box. As you did with the poppet, tie
the twine and seal it with the black wax. Melt whatever is
left from the black candle onto the twine and box.

Safeguard this in a closet or other out of the way place.
Putting it in the back of your refrigerator is a nice gesture—
a freezer is even better—but if you want to really do it
right, dig a hole in the ground where you are sure it will
not be disturbed. Throw the box into the hole as if to cast
off the person's influence. Cast the remnants of anything
you used for this spell into the hole. A final and most
appropriate gesture is to urinate into the hole, casting off
the person's magick the way you cast off last night's beer.
Fill in the hole. Watch the sunset and visualize the person's
magickal energy fade the way the sun fades.

A Spell to Attract Money

MATERIALS: 3 small pieces of green paper (two- to three-inch squares)
2 tablespoons nutmeg
1 tablespoon cinnamon
1 green candle
4 tablespoons patchouly
1 twenty-dollar bill (larger denomination is fine)
1 green cloth (about five inches square)
Money-drawing oil or essential oil of patchouly
1 coin (real silver or gold)
1 gold-colored ribbon (nine inches)

TOOLS: Gold pen or gold paint and brush
Mortar and pestle
Matches or a lighter
Fire-safe container

Arrange a table so that as you face it you are facing southwest. If using a gold pen it should be placed on the right. If using gold paint and a brush, the paint should be on the left and the brush on the right. The mortar should be on the left and the pestle on the right. In the center on separate small pieces of green paper, place each herb. All remaining items go in the center of the table

Spinning the Spell

This spell is best spun on Thursday during the first hour of Jupiter (see page 49). Anoint the candle with the oil and then light it. One at a time, add each of the three herbs to the mortar. Place the green papers that the herbs were on aside. You will use them later. Take the mortar in your left hand and the pestle in your right. Grind and blend the three herb mixture until it has the uniform consistency of a powder. As you grind, visualize your essence leaving your right hand and being projected into the herbs through the pestle.

Draw a dollar sign or other symbol of wealth on each of the three pieces of green paper. Place the twenty-dollar bill on top of the green cloth. Place three pinches of the herb mixture onto each piece of paper and then three drops money-drawing oil or patchouly essential to each. The remaining mixture is poured onto the twenty-dollar bill and topped with an equal amount of oil, and then with the coin. Pull the sides of the cloth up so that the edges meet at the top and form a bag. Close it with the gold-colored ribbon, making sure to wrap it nine times. Seal the knot by dripping nine drops of wax from the green candle onto the knot. Fold each of the three pieces of green paper so that the dollar sign is on the inside and the herb mixture is contained. Seal the paper shut with three drops of wax on each. Put out the candle and save it for later.

During the first hour of Jupiter on each Thursday for the next three weeks, place one of the folded pieces of paper into a fire-safe container and burn it. You can drip some more wax from the green candle on the paper to get it to burn better. Allow the flame and embers to go out naturally. As the smoke rises, visualize your prayers rising to deity as a petition. Carry the green bag with you until you receive some surprise income. When you do, remove the paper money from the bag and give it to your favorite charity. Keep the coin with you for luck. Fashion it into jewelry if you are able. Burn the remnants of the bag and herbs in a fire.

A Spell for Home Protection
(Making a "Witches' Bottle")

MATERIALS: Salt (a few teaspoons)
       3 cloves garlic
       3 teaspoons asafetida
       3 whole bay leaves

> 1 glass jar or bottle with wide mouth and good
>   sealing top
> Thorns gathered specifically for this purpose
> Small pieces of accidentally broken glass or mirror
> A full bladder
> Water, if needed
> Wax, for sealing the bottle

OPTIONAL: One teaspoon of any three of these herbs can be
>   substituted for the asafetida: basil, dill, sage,
>   anise, black pepper, or fennel
>   Red food coloring
>   A small bottle
>   A piece of cord

If you cannot find asafetida, or you already know what it smells like and would like to avoid it, pick three of the alternative herbs listed and use one teaspoon of each. If you have never used asafetida, let me warn you in advance that its smell is so bad that one sniff has been known to cause people to become ill.

Do not break glass or mirrors intentionally for this spell. It is best that you save broken glass from your own mishaps, but collecting glass from others' mistakes is fine. For personal protection, it is acceptable to use a small bottle and string it on a cord to make a necklace. Read the entire spell before you decide if it is a good idea for you.

Spinning the Spell

This spell is best if completed just before the sunrise on a Thursday. Add the salt, garlic, and herbs to the bottle one at a time. Do not crush the herbs if you do not have to. Add thorns and broken bits of glass or mirror. If you happen to cut yourself, allow your blood to drip into the bottle as well. Do not intentionally cut yourself for this purpose. I have found that a particularly strong bottle can be had if you get the bottle ready, but only add accidental blood and broken glass as they make themselves available. With a two-thousand-square-foot workshop, lots of sharp tools, and the dexterity of an urban Yeti, or "Bigfoot," obtaining accidental blood takes me about a week and a half. Empty your bladder into the bottle. Top the bottle with water if necessary. Adding red food coloring is a nice touch. Firmly seal the bottle. If you use a cork, seal it with wax.

Put the bottle in a place where it will be struck by the sun from sunrise to sunset. Warning: It is entirely possible that this bottle will explode. Make sure it is placed where it will neither be disturbed nor pose a health threat. Just before the next sunrise, retrieve the bottle and place it on your front porch. Make sure it is in a safe location. If you vent the top of the bottle, you can prevent the bottle from bursting, but the liquid contents will evaporate. Besides, a little explosion is sometimes a fun thing. It lets you know it's time to make a new Witches' bottle.

12

Creation's Covenant's Book of Shadows

What follows in this chapter is a portion of the working Book of Shadows (B.O.S.) of Creation's Covenant. It contains a self-dedication rite and group celebrations for each of the eight sabbats. The group celebrations can be easily modified for solitary practitioners. Much time and consideration has been taken to connect each ritual with those further along on the wheel of the year. Such consistency has been maintained to keep the wheel in motion in our psyche the way it is in nature. None of these rituals stand alone. Like an eight-spoke wheel, removing even one spoke will throw off the balance.

These rituals are based on some of the material that was presented in chapter 8. Remember that there is a wealth of information available on which to base your celebrations. It is also important to remember that these are merely the rituals that take place during a celebration. They are no more the whole of the celebration than the wedding is the whole of a marriage. Celebration takes place during the preparation of and after the ritual, the same way families gather before and host a reception after a wedding. Although alcohol is ill advised before ritual and never mandated during or after ritual celebration, Creation's Covenant encourages merriment at times of celebration. If alcohol is consumed at any point in one of our rituals, it is mandated that the host(s) provide transportation or sleeping arrangements to anyone who indulges.

As with all celebrations, these rites should be considered joyous occasions. Avoid falling into the trap laid by more traditional religions. Religion should not be stuffy.

A Self-Dedication Ritual

Self-dedication should not be confused with initiation. A self-dedication is a declaration to yourself. It states that you are committed to follow the path to which you are dedicating yourself. This is witnessed by the Gods and Goddesses but no one else.

For this rite, you will need only the chalice (filled with red wine or juice) and the athame. A symbol of your devotion such as a necklace or a ring is a good idea. If it is a ring, it should be worn on the ring (third) finger of your right hand. If it is a necklace, it is best if the necklace has no clasp. Each of these symbols reflects the union of male and female when it is place on the body. I think the ring is the better idea as this rite can be considered a symbol of engagement to deity.

Find a comfortable place and time for your dedication. Ensure that you will not be disturbed. Although the scripted part of the dedication does not take a lot of time, you will be meditating during this rite. Dedicants often report a great amount of time passing during their commitment meditation. Some report feeling divine intervention at that point, so allow extra time.

Creation's Covenant does not stress ritual nudity for any rite other than the self-dedication. Your self-dedication rite is your birth into this tradition. As you came into this world clad only by the sky, you can only come into this tradition skyclad. If you have a problem being naked in front of yourself, you should seek professional counseling.

Your body should not be decorated with any jewelry— you should not be wearing your necklace or ring at this point. Likewise, there should be nothing within your circle except the athame, chalice of wine, and symbol of your devotion. There should be nothing to distract you.

Sit in the center of what will be your circle. Place the athame, chalice, and devotion symbol in front of you. Meditate on what is about to take place. This is not a decision you should make lightly. If you were raised in a traditional Western religion, you are about to throw away the religion of your parents and their parents. You will be committing yourself to see the value in all life, male and female. Living in a culture where God is traditionally male, this decision is the difference between a sole proprietorship and a partnership.

When you are ready, stand and lift the athame with your right hand. Hold it horizontally to the sky in an open hand, as if to present it to your father who is observing this rite from above. In similar words, but from the heart: "Father, I use this tool in your many names to carve a sacred space for this rite." Stand in silence until you feel the moment is right, then go to the easternmost part of your circle. Point the athame at the ground. Visualize the energy from your God entering your body from above and leaving through the athame. Continue the visualization as you move clockwise around the circle back to east. Return to the center of the circle. Hold the athame horizontally in an open hand. Kneel and hold it just above the ground as if to present it to your mother, who is watching this rite from below. In similar words, but from the heart: "Mother, I use this tool in your many names to carve a sacred space for this rite." Kneel in silence until you feel the moment is right, then go to the easternmost part of your circle. Point the athame at the sky. Visualize the energy from your Goddess entering your body from below and leaving through the athame. Continue the visualization as you move clockwise around the circle back to east. Return to the center of the circle. The circle is now cast.

Face East: "I call the forces of air and invite them to become the breath of the Wiccan who is born here tonight."

Face South: "I call the forces of fire and invite them to become the spirit of the Wiccan who is born here tonight."

Face West: "I call the forces of water and invite them to become the blood of the Wiccan who is born here tonight."

Face North: "I call the forces of earth and invite them to become the body of the Wiccan who is born here tonight."

Hold the athame in your right hand and the chalice in your left. Know that this is the first secret of Creation's Covenant, that we are separated for the sake of union. In your own words, invite your God to enter the circle and to unite through athame and chalice with your Goddess. In your own words, invite your Goddess to enter the circle and to unite through chalice and athame with your God. Lower the blade of the athame into the chalice. You are now Wiccan, born in the union of that symbolic great rite.

Drink the wine knowing that it the fruit of their union. Don the symbol.

If you have read this book and feel it is the right path for you, you may now consider yourself a member of Creation's Covenant's outer circle.

The Sabbat Rituals of Creation's Covenant

(Note: These rites are written for group worship but can easily be modified for solitary practitioners.)

A Ritual for Samhain

Timing: I have found that the Samhain ritual is best per- formed at night.

Preparation: A table additional to the main altar is placed within the circle. This is known as the remembrance altar. Here should be placed the favored meals, drinks, pho- tos, and other items of remembrance for loved ones who have crossed. Tools of divination, especially scrying bowls and mirrors, should also be placed on the remembrance altar. Larger scrying tools, such as cauldrons filled with water, should be placed in the center of the circle. If neces- sary, move the main altar a bit to the east to make room for large scrying devices. Extra black candles should be available for each person in attendance. All the necessary service items (plates, spoons) are on the remembrance altar along with an extra glass and plate.

Masks of attributes participants wish to cast off should be worn into circle. Masks of attributes participants desire should be placed on the main altar or the quarter altars. Try to pick the altar best associated with the symbolism of the mask. If you wish to bring Fire energy into your life, place the mask on the Fire altar. If you are attempting to better connect with your feminine side, place it on the Goddess half of the main altar.

If this is an indoor ritual, there should be a wood or cardboard box just outside the gate. Outdoors, it is better to have a small fire just outside the gate. If a new broom was made for this occasion, it should be placed on or leaning against the God side of the main altar.

Everyone in attendance should make an effort to bring one canned good or nonperishable food item. If nonperishables were collected at the Autumn Equinox, those food items should be placed on the harvest altar prior to the ritual.

The Ritual: After the temple is erected as discussed in chapter 8, the Priest speaks. This task can fall on the Priestess if you like, but the Priest is more appropriate for this task, as he represents the dwindling sun approaching death and rebirth.

Priest: "This is the time of death. It is the time between worlds. It is a time for forgetting and of letting go."

The Priest instructs those standing to either side of the gate to open it. The Priest walks through the gate to the fire or box. There he announces the symbolism of the mask he has worn into ritual. He removes it and destroys it in some manner. Simply tearing it in half will do. He then casts the remnants of the mask into the fire or box. As the Priest is doing this, the Priestess gathers all who have masks to discard. She sends them through the gate one at a time to meet with the Priest, who removes the mask and asks what the mask that is to be destroyed represents. He then says, "I am your dying God bringing that which you wish dead with me." After he destroys each mask in similar fashion, the unmasked member of the circle returns to his or her place in the circle. Once the last mask is destroyed, the Priest reenters the circle and the gate is closed.

Priestess: "This is the third harvest. It is a time to set aside food for the cold winter ahead. If you have brought offerings of nonperishable food, please bring them forward."

The cans and nonperishables are collected and placed on the harvest altar.

Priestess: "This is a time of rebirth and of the new year. It is the time between worlds. It is a time of remembrance and of forgiveness. It is a time to feast with our ancestors."

As the Priestess approaches the remembrance altar, she asks everyone to sit. She then picks items on the altar one at a time, calling forth the one who brought the items into the circle, beginning with the food items. The person who brought the dish informs the circle of its origin and the loved one to whom it is connected. Any pictures or other remembrances of that loved one are shared as the dish is shared by all. Exceptions can always be made by vegetarians and those who have deep convictions against certain foods. Trivial distaste should be overlooked as it is offensive. From each dish, a portion is placed on the extra plate. From each drink, a portion is added to the extra cup. Each time a picture or other remembrance is shown, it is placed on the main altar. This way the Priestess can keep track of what is left in the remembrance. Once all meals have been consumed and all items on the remembrance table have been explained, shared, and placed on the main altar, the gate is again opened and the Priestess carries the extra plate and cup to a point just outside the gate.

Priestess: "This is for my ancestors and for my missing loved ones. Behold! Here is your favorite food and drink combined with those favored by the ancestors and missing loved ones of my Wiccan brothers and sisters. Enjoy them together as we have and become family with each other as we have."

The Priestess reenters the circle and does what some might think unspeakable. After she enters the circle she turns and stops those who hold open the gate from closing it. At this point she takes the broom and announces that the circle remains open for our ancestors to join us. The broom is then set aside or broken over her knee and cast outside of the circle. If you like the theatrics of breaking the broom, you might want to cut the handle part way through ahead of time. Breaking the broom should *not* be done unless another one is ready to replace it during the latter part of this rite. Ceremonial magickians and the truly paranoid can entirely ignore this practice out of sheer fear of what might enter the circle. The mildly concerned may wish to ward the gate with pentagrams or other devices designed to keep mischievous and baneful influences out, while allowing ancestral spirits in.

The Priest then leads the group in divination. In some groups this will take the form of group divination around a central scrying device or into individual bowls illuminated by individual black candles. Groups who are comfortable with different forms of divination can trade skills, reading tarot or runes for each other. The key to this practice is to share insight into the new year. Everyone should feel comfortable to speak his or her mind and tell the group what he or she sees.

Once everyone has concluded his or her divination, the Priestess thanks the ancestral spirits, telling them that she is now going to close the gate but assuring them that they are welcome to "stay if you will, but go if you must." The gate is then closed by lowering the new broom onto the gate stones.

The Priestess then goes to the East altar. If there is a mask there, she inquires to whom it belongs, then brings the mask to its owner and asks him or her to tell the group what the mask represents. Once finished, the Priestess helps the circle member don the mask. As she does, she says, "I am the forever living Goddess, here forever to help you bring these attributes into your life." She addresses each mask on each altar one at a time, first at the East altar, then moving clockwise through the South, West, and North altars. Once all the masks are gone from the quarter altars, she does the same with the masks on the main altar and finally dons her own mask.

The circle is closed in the manner discussed in chapter 7. Activities after a Samhain ritual usually include further divination. Remembrances after the ritual need not be somber. I am sure my father appreciates my remembering him with an Irish wake attitude. If you enjoyed some of the dishes that you were served, ask for the recipes and be prepared to share recipes should you be asked. If there is a kitchen available, teach each other the recipes throughout the night. If you just can't eat any more, prepare the dishes and bring them home to loved ones who could not be at the celebration. The nonperishable food should be given to anyone in the circle who honestly needs it. Otherwise, give it to a local shelter.

A Ritual for the Winter Solstice

Timing: I have found that the Winter Solstice ritual is best if the preparations begin in the late morning hours of the day of the solstice. This way, if guests want to drum up the returning solstice sun they can arrive just before sunrise, drum in the sun, and then help with preparation.

Preparation: A Yule tree is placed in the center of the circle. If need be, the main altar can be moved slightly to the east and the Yule tree placed slightly to the west. It should be a living tree potted so that it can be easily transplanted in the spring. The size is dependent on your budget and space accommodations. Acquire trees only from nurseries. Do not remove a tree from nature, which would be redundant as it is going to be planted at Summer Solstice. If gifts are to be exchanged, they should be arranged around the Yule tree. If the tree is to be decorated, the decorations should be placed appropriately on the quarter altars. Use the color and nature of the ornament to decide on which quarter altar they belong.

If you saved a single green sachet of ashes gathered at Bealtaine, place them on the Goddess side of the main altar. If circle members have also saved ashes from Bealtaines past, they should keep them with them during this rite.

Two Priests are needed for this rite as it involves the sacred play of the conflict between the Oak King and the Holly King. The Priest who will represent the Oak King should wait outside of circle in a separate room or behind a black veil. He should have with him a candelabra of yellow or gold candles (preferably twelve) and a sword or staff. Making an Oak King crown with oak leaves and a Holly King crown with holly leaves is a good idea. Give them to those who will play the roles. They should wear them during ritual.

A dish of sun cakes and/or cookies should be placed on the God half of the main altar. Round cakes and cheeses are also welcome as are drinks befitting the sun, like orange juice. The cakes and cheese can be sliced into eighths to symbolize the Wheel of the Year. Foods set aside during the last two harvests should also be present. Other foods symbolic of the sun are welcome and should come from as many circle members as are willing to contribute. Preparing these foods can be part of the pre-ritual fun.

The Ritual: The temple is erected as discussed in chapter 8 except the Great Rite should not be performed at this point. The room should remain completely dark except for the candles that were lit during the erecting of the temple.

Priest: "I am the Holly King, the old and waning sun. I welcome my death that I will be reborn in light."

The Priest then moves to the gate and lifts the broom (or second sword if available) from the gate stones. He shakes the broom, which should be laced with bells. He takes several steps backward, then kneels with his arms holding the broom over his head as if to parry a blow from an unseen attack. The Oak King, having taken his cue from the bells, approaches the gate with candelabra lit and held in one hand, the sword or staff ready in the other. He enters through the gate and stops directly in front of the kneeling Holly King. The Holly King willingly lays the broom at the feet of the Oak King. The Oak King lightly taps the Holly King on the head with the flat of his sword. The Holly King falls limp. The Priestess, in her role as Goddess, kneels at the Holly King's side, and mourns the passing of her fallen Lord.

The Oak King places the candelabra on the God side of the altar. He then places the sword on the God half of the main altar and the broom on the gate stones to close the gate. He then takes the chalice of wine in his left hand and the athame in his right. He offers the chalice to the still-kneeling Priestess. The symbolic Great Rite is performed. The Oak King returns the athame, then helps the Holly King to his feet. They embrace as brothers. The Priestess offers the chalice of wine to the Holly King first, then the circle, herself, and finally the Oak King. The Oak and Holly King then invite the circle to join in the feast of the new sun. Both Oak King and Holly King pass food and drink to the circle. It is most appropriate to sit after this sacred play to enjoy the meal, but not before.

During the meal, the Priestess goes first to the East altar and holds up each Yule tree decoration, asking who brought it and what its significance is. Then she invites the one who brought it to add it to the Yule tree. She does this with each ornament on each altar, moving clockwise.

Once the tree is decorated and the meal is complete, the green sachets of Bealtaine fire ash are offered to the tree. Presents are exchanged and explained. Even if a gift exchange was worked out it is a good idea for the Priest and Priestess to cooperatively arrange for an additional gift to be available for all in attendance as well as any surprise guests. It is also customary for each member to give a gift to the coven in care of the Priest and Priestess. These are most often wine, candles, and other items for use in future rituals. Remember that although your Priest and Priestess are your hosts, operating a coven does come with an expense account. Any effort at replenishing coven supplies will lessen their burden.

The circle is closed in the manner discussed in chapter 7. This is often followed by caroling and other merriment. For a good listing of Pagan songs, you need only examine the words to traditional carols of the season. Especially with "Deck the Halls," you will find that the majority still hold true to their Pagan origins. Be inventive and change the words of traditional songs. Most of them were Pagan long before they were Christianized so don't feel guilty about embellishment. It's not an act of theft, its an act of reclamation.

A Ritual for Imbolg

Timing: I have found that the Imbolg ritual goes best if started in late afternoon or early evening.

Preparation: A large basket of the craft supplies necessary for this rite should sit at the center of the circle. If space dictates, move the main altar slightly east and place the basket slightly west. In and around the basket should be the makings of both a phallic wand and a corn doll. If there are women in your group who are capable of weaving material saved from Lughnasadh into a second basket, make sure the materials are available. If that skill is not present among the womenfolk, make sure you have an empty basket. If you have saved a corn doll from Lughnasadh, place it in the basket along with beads and shells to decorate it. Nuts, acorns, and other naturally phallic items should also be placed in the basket, especially those found and saved during Bealtaine nut hunts.

The Ritual: The temple is erected as discussed in chapter 7, except that the last act of erecting the temple at Imbolg is to invite the Lord and Lady. The Great Rite is postponed until later in the ritual. The Priest and Priestess invite the circle members to join them around the baskets. They should form a half circle of men and a half circle of women. All sit facing the basket, the men on the God half of the circle with their backs to the east and south quarters and the women on the Goddess half of the circle with their backs to the west and north quarters.

As the Priest leads the men in the construction and decoration of a phallic wand to represent Lord, the Priestess leads the womenfolk in the creation and/or the decoration of the corn doll to represent Lady. If you prefer, a corn doll to represent the Lord can be fabricated instead of the phallic wand. If there is a second basket, it should be decorated similarly to the Lady doll because it will be her bed. If not, the basket is woven from the available material. There is no need to rush this activity. With the realization that the objects are being personified as lovers, the conversations should prove interesting. If conversation does not follow this path, or even if it does, "Bardic lubrication" is welcome if all have consented previously. (By the way, Bardic lubrication is a reference to wine, ale, or other similarly intoxicating substances.)

When the men and women are finished with the basket, Lady doll, and phallic wand or Lord doll, everyone stands again. The basket that symbolizes the Lady's bed is placed on the center of the main altar. The Lady doll is placed on the Goddess half of the main altar and the symbol that was made to represent the Lord is placed on the God side of the altar. The Priest and Priestess then arrange the circle into a male, female, male, female order. If you have more of one sex, just approximate.

The Priestess takes the chalice of wine in her left hand and the Lady doll in her right. The Priest takes the athame in the right hand and the Lord symbol (doll or phallic wand) in his left. The symbolic Great Rite is performed by the Priest and Priestess and the Lord and Lady symbols are placed in the basket. With the basket held by the left hand of the Priest and the right hand of the Priestess, the couple go to the gate. The gate is then opened by both the Priest and Priestess. The Priestess lifts the broom from the left using her left hand and the Priest from the right using his right hand.

The Priest and Priestess then leave the circle with the basket and close the gate behind them. They go to a secluded place where they meditate on the conception of the land. If the Priest and Priestess are lovers who wish to conceive a child, it is most appropriate for them to consummate the union of Lord and Lady with the actual Great Rite.

If there is a couple other than the Priest and Priestess who would like to consummate the union of the Lord and Lady, the Priest and Priestess should give the basket to that couple. If there are additional couples, use the time the first couple is away to make additional sets. As the couple(s) meditate or make love in relative seclusion, the rest of the group may drum slowly, sing, and take part in other merriment. When the couple feels the spark of life has entered Goddess, they should return in modest fashion and announce that the spark of life has entered the Goddess. The actual wording should be from the heart and can come from different couples at different times should several couples be used. I strongly suggest that lovers who do not wish to conceive on this night refrain from consummating the evening even if they take modern birth control measures.

Once all members of the circle have returned, the circle is closed in the manner discussed in chapter 7. Lounging after this celebration is most common. Lovers are more than welcome to find their own sacred places for further celebration. Couples that did not want to be obvious are welcome to visit the room where the Lady and Lord symbols were put to bed. Some groups might not feel the seclusion necessary, but such openness is recommended only if all present are comfortable with the terms of the openness. As with all Wiccan rites, none should be made uncomfortable by majority opinion.

A Ritual for the Spring Equinox

Timing: There is no best time to perform this ritual.
Preparation: Hard-boiled eggs and supplies with which to decorate the eggs should be at hand. If you made a bas-

ket at Imbolg, it is very appropriate to use that basket to hold the eggs. Flower pots and potting soil should be on the Goddess side of the altar. Seeds should be on the God side of the altar. A watering can should sit on the floor outside of the circle. Other food and drink to amply feed all in attendance can be placed here as well.

The Ritual: The temple is erected as discussed in chapter 8 except that the symbolic Great Rite is not performed during the raising of the temple. The Priest and Priestess separate the men and women into two groups. The women fill a flower pot for each female in the circle, including the Priestess. A small indentation should be made in the potting soil for the seeds. The Priest counts out nine seeds into each man's right hand. The Priest should be sure that there are ample seeds left should there be more women than men as it will be his responsibility to provide seeds to an odd number. These extra seeds should be placed on the God side of the altar. Each woman carries a filled flower pot, except the Priestess, who places hers on the Goddess half of the altar. The Priest and Priestess then guide the group back into a circle. Try to stick to a male, female, male, female order as much as possible. If you have an unequal number of each sex, approximate.

The Priestess then selects women from the circle one at a time. She asks each woman if there is a man in the circle whose seed is right for her earth. If the answer is the name of the Priest, she is brought to the Goddess side of the altar and told to wait. If the answer is the name of any other man in the circle, the man is called forth. The gate is opened and the couple is told to plant their seed. The couples leave one at a time and may return one at a time. If there are women who have run out of men from which to choose, or if they have chosen the Priest, he accommodates.

The reverse is true with uncoupled men and the Priestess. However, there can be no time when neither the Priest nor Priestess are in the circle.

Once the Priest's or Priestess's duties in the planting matters have been completed, they should sit in the middle of the circle and lead everyone in decorating the eggs. You should not wait for everyone to return from the chore of planting as some may take much longer than others. As each couple returns, the group welcomes them and invites them to rejoin the circle. When everyone is back in the circle, a break in the egg decorating is taken. Everyone stands and reforms the circle.

The Priestess then takes the chalice of wine in her left hand and the flower pot in the right. The Priest takes the athame in the right hand and the seeds in his left. The symbolic Great Rite is performed and the seeds are added to the potting soil. The Priest and Priestess welcome everyone to continue to decorate the eggs and dine on the egg feast as they leave to plant their seeds. Slow drumming and gentle chants are a good form of entertainment at this point. The feast continues until the Priest and Priestess return.

As the earth in the pot represents the womb of the land, so does the woman carrying the earth represent the Goddess. As the seed in the men's hands represents the seed of God, so does the man represent God. With this in mind, you can see that while each couple is planting their seeds, the actual Great Rite is not only welcome but highly appropriate. The time that can be involved in the Great Rite is why the feast is started before everyone returns.

Once all members of the circle have returned, the circle is closed in the manner discussed in chapter 8. The after-ritual activities are similar to those after Imbolg.

A Ritual for Bealtaine

Timing: I have found that the Bealtaine rite is best if started just past sunset. This way the festivities can go on until sunrise.

Preparation: A main altar is not used at Bealtaine. The four primary ritual tools are returned to the quarter altars as they are used. The salt tile is placed on the Fire altar and the water dish is placed on the Water altar. Other items are placed on the quarter altars with similar correspondence. Green sachets or pieces of cloth and ribbons are placed on the Earth altar. One piece of black cloth should be placed on each quarter altar. Rattles, pairs of hardwood rods, and other simple noise makers should be placed on the Air altar.

This celebration will take the entire night, so large amounts of food and drink are advised. Extra wine, juice, and water should be placed on the Water altar. Grains, breads, and cakes should be placed on the Earth altar. The Air and Fire altars can be stocked with foods that correspond by color. Drummers should carry their drums into circle and keep them with them.

The circle area should be much larger than normal. In its center, a pit should be dug for the Bel-fire. Stone circles also keep the fire from spreading, but if you intend on leaping the flames, using a fire pit will lower the wood and lessen the chances of someone getting hurt. (Our bodies tend to pass through flame with much less resistance than they pass through wood. Still, this practice always has the chance of injury. Several years back, an officer in a Pagan networking group broke his leg while leaping a fire. That organization later banned the practice at their events.)

The Ritual: The Bel-fire is lit before the temple is erected. With only a few differences, the temple is then erected as explained in chapter 7. At Bealtaine, there is no need to light a work candle as the Bel-fire itself is the work candle. God and Goddess candles and images are not used at Bealtaine because the central focus of this celebration is human fertility and sexuality. The God image is each man in the circle; the Goddess image is each woman in the circle. After the salted water is used to spurge the group, the salted water is cast into the Bel-fire. Likewise, after the incense is used, the remnants of the incense and charcoal are thrown into the Bel-fire. After each of the main ritual tools is used, it is returned to the appropriate altar and wrapped in the black cloth.

At Bealtaine, the symbolic Great Rite should be more graphic. The Priestess should lay on the earth with her chalice elevated above her lower abdomen and her legs spread. The Priest should kneel between her legs with the athame over the chalice. As he lowers the athame into the chalice, the words to describe the act of union should come from his heart. The Priest returns the athame to the Fire altar and retrieves a bottle of wine from the Water altar. The Priestess brings the chalice to the East Quarter to share the wine. She moves clockwise, sharing the wine with each person in attendance. The Priest follows her. After each tilting of the chalice, the Priestess holds the chalice to just below her waist and the Priest refills it. If the bottle runs dry, the Priest retrieves a new one.

After one full circle has been made with the wine, the Priest announces that the drumming may begin. A second circle with the wine is made in like fashion to the first. After the second full circle has been made with the wine, the Priestess announces that the dancing may begin. Dancers should move closer to the fire and dance, moving clockwise around the pit. If there is anyone still in the outer circle who is not drumming, a third circle with the wine should be poured. This time, give anyone who is not drumming a noisemaker to keep the beat.

The Priest and Priestess remove the broom from the gate and announce that "The circle is open but left unbroken." If for any reason someone wants to leave the circle, they should do so through the gate. The Priest and Priestess join in the revelry but retain their positions as hosts. Those who invited the quarters are charged with distributing all the food and drink except the wine and alcohol. The decision to distribute more alcohol is the responsibility of the Priest and Priestess, but this decision does not need to be made for each glass. Eating and drinking should be conducted at the outer circle so as to not interfere with the dancers.

Bealtaine Games

More than any other celebration, Bealtaine is a time of lover's games. I have always been fond of the kissing game. The following three games have been played to great success. Use one or all three.

1. The kissing game starts with an orange. Dozens of cloves are pressed into the orange and it is passed from man to woman or woman to man. The recipient accepts the orange and removes one of the cloves with his or her teeth. The clove is chewed and the two kiss. The recipient of the orange is then free to give the orange to another, who responds in kind.

2. The nut hunt is a good game for this celebration. In this game, women will leave the circle and gather nuts (symbols of male vitality) in the woods. Presenting them to a suitable man in the circle is a clear way of showing their intentions. Casting the nuts into the fire and releasing

their energy by flame is a way of casting your desire for a love to the four winds. Place a few of the nuts aside for use in the Winter Solstice rite. Men can seek the affection of women in the same way, only that the men should collect flowers (symbols of female fertility).

3. The maypole dance is one of the most traditional ways of celebrating this holiday. The pole itself is clearly a phallic symbol. The dancers weave cloth around the pole to form a symbolic vaginal tunnel around the phallic symbol. The maypole should always be arranged in the center of the circle. If you choose to use one, move the Bel-fire location more to the east and the maypole to the south. The pole should be long and sturdy enough that once it is sunk into the ground, at least nine feet will remain above ground. Three-inch-wide strips of fabric or strong ribbon should be attached at the top. The length of the fabric should be at least one quarter longer than the length of the pole. Alternate the colors of the fabric between red and white, with an equal number of red and white ribbons. The dance starts with the men holding the end of the red ribbons and the women holding the white. The ribbons are stretched outward such that the shape of a cone or an umbrella is achieved. Women stand facing their partner (if available) with their right shoulder toward the pole. The men stand facing their partner (if available) with their left shoulder toward the pole.

Drumming and chanting gives the dancers their cue. The dance begins with the men moving counterclockwise and the women moving clockwise. As people pass, they weave in and out, causing the ribbons to also weave in and out. As the dance continues, the woven part of the ribbon becomes longer and longer, starting at the top. The unwoven part becomes shorter and shorter. The symbolism here is the lowering of the vagina onto the phallus. As the unwoven portion of the ribbons shorten, the dancers are drawn closer and closer to the pole and to each other. When there is no more ribbon or pole (depending on the tightness of the weave) the ends of the cord are nailed, tied, or otherwise affixed to the pole.

In the morning, ashes from the Bel-fire are gathered and placed in the green sachets. These sachets are given as mementos of the evening and fertility talismans to all who remain. The gate is closed and the ritual is ended in the manner discussed in chapter 8. The after-ritual celebration usually includes making sure the Bel-fire coals have turned to cold ash, which is frequently scattered on crops. The most common after-Bealtaine ritual merriment is to fall asleep in your lover's arms.

✗

A Ritual for the Summer Solstice

Timing: I have found that the Summer Solstice ritual is best if the preparations and revelry begin at high afternoon hours to celebrate the height of the sun on its longest day. The rite itself is best received when set against the setting sun. The celebration is of the turning of the wheel. At this point, the wheel is turning toward darkness.

Preparation: This rite involves the planting of a tree or other hardy perennial. The best choice is the Yule tree from the Winter Solstice ritual. An appropriate-sized hole should be dug where the tree will be planted, which is best if it is within the circle. Next to the hole, set a watering can or vase of water. The candelabra used at Winter Solstice should rest on the God half of the main altar. A sword or staff is needed. Crowns similar to those used at Winter Solstice are suggested.

This rite is very similar to the Winter Solstice ritual. Two Priests are needed for this rite. One will represent the Oak King and one the Holly King. At this rite, the one who will represent the Holly King should wait outside the circle. He should have with him the same sword or staff that was used in the Winter Solstice rite. If there is a member of the circle who is pregnant and the Priestess is not, the role of Priestess should be given to the pregnant woman for this rite—but only if the Priestess feels it is appropriate and the substitute is suited for the role.

A dish of sun cakes and/or cookies should be placed on the God half of the main altar: Round cakes and cheeses are also welcome as are drinks befitting the sun, like orange juice. The cakes and cheeses can be sliced into eighths to symbolize the wheel of the year. By serving foods similar to what is served at Winter Solstice, a connection will be formed. This will enhance future Winter Solstice rites as the promise of the sun's return will be linked to the warmth experienced during the Summer Solstice ritual. Foods set aside during the last two harvests should also be present. Other foods symbolic of the sun are welcome and should come from as many circle members as are willing to contribute. Preparing these foods can be part of the preritual fun.

The Ritual: The temple is erected as discussed in chapter 8, except that the symbolic Great Rite is not performed at first. The candelabra that was used during the Winter Solstice ritual should be lit instead of the God candle. Outside the circle, perhaps hidden behind a tree, the Holly King waits with sword at the ready.

The Priest (Oak King) removes the tree from its container and lowers it into the ground. He then begins pushing the dirt that was removed to make the hole back into the hole.

Priestess: "Even at the last moments of his life, our beloved Oak King provides for us. We should help him with his labors."

The Priestess leads the circle members in helping the Oak King plant the tree. The circle members kneel and cast the dirt into the hole until the tree is planted. Once the tree is firmly planted, all members of the group return to their places in circle.

Priest (Oak King): "I am the Oak King, the old waxing sun. I welcome my death knowing that I will be reborn in darkness."

The Priest extinguishes each candle in the candelabra one at a time. He then moves to the gate and lifts the broom from the gate stones. He shakes the broom, which should be laced with bells. He takes several steps backward, then kneels with his arms holding the broom over his head as if to parry a blow from an unseen attack.

The Holly King, having taken his cue from the bells, approaches the gate with the sword or staff ready. The Holly King enters through the gate and stops directly in front of the kneeling Oak King. The Oak King then willingly lays the broom at the feet of the Holly King. The Holly King lightly taps the Oak King on the head with the flat of his sword. The Oak King falls limp. The Priestess, in her role as Goddess, kneels at the Oak King's side and mourns the passing of her fallen Lord.

The Holly King places the sword on the God side of the altar, then replaces the broom on the gate stones to close the gate. He then takes the chalice of wine in his left hand and the athame in his right hand. He offers the chalice to the still kneeling Priestess and the symbolic Great Rite is performed. The Holly King returns the athame, then helps the Oak King to his feet. They embrace as brothers. The Priestess offers the chalice of wine to the Oak King. He drinks and returns the chalice to the Priestess. The Oak King then hands the watering pot to the Holly King. The Holly King waters the tree as the Priestess shares the wine with those in the circle, she drinks some herself, and finally she shares it with the Holly King. The Holly King and the Oak King then invite the circle to join in the feast of the new sun. Both the Holy King and the Oak King pass food and drink to the circle. It is most appropriate to sit after this sacred play to enjoy the meal, but not before.

Drumming, dancing, and general merriment is more than welcome during the meal and should continue into the night even once the rite is over. The circle is closed in the manner discussed in chapter 8.

A Ritual for Lughnasadh

Timing: There is no best time to perform this ritual.

Preparation: An additional altar, the harvest altar, should be placed in the center of the circle. If necessary, place the main altar a bit to the east and the harvest altar a bit to the west. The harvest altar should be low enough to the ground so that one can sit on the ground but feel comfortable working at the table. If a table is not available, spread a cloth on the ground. Items necessary to make a broom (besom) should be placed on the harvest altar along with corn husks and silks. Use the preparation time to both boil corn for the feast and arrange the husks and silks on the altar.

A cornucopia (horn of plenty) should rest on the harvest altar. Food and drink, also on the harvest altar, should be in large supply. Corn, wheat, and other grains of the area should be predominant for the feast. If you have a garden of your own, early harvests are also good. (Many tomatoes and squash plants will fruit in time for this celebration.)

Artisans and crafters are encouraged to bring the fruits of their creativity to this celebration. Their art work should be displayed on the main altar and around the elemental altars suitable to each symbolic association. For example, pottery, which is formed of earth, should be set on or near the Earth altar. If the artisans and crafters would like to share projects with the group, they should be prepared to do so.

The Ritual: The temple is erected as discussed in chapter 7. The Priest gathers the men to the harvest altar, where they begin making the broom which will replace the one that is destroyed at Samhain. The Priestess leads the women of the circle to the harvest altar, where each is led in making corn dolls. It is acceptable and common for folk to sit around the harvest altar for this portion of the rite. When finished, everyone stands and takes their place in the circle. The Priest places the broom on the God half of the main altar; the Priestess places her corn doll on the Goddess side.

Priest: "This is the time of the first harvest, but without sacrifice there would be no feast. As our sun has sacrificed himself for this feast, so have we sacrificed our labors for the meal. Now that our harvest is full, it is time for our bellies to be full."

The Priest and Priestess lead the feast. During the feast, the Priest and Priestess should prompt the artisans and crafters to explain their displayed works and involve others in ongoing projects. The kissing game, described in the Bealtaine rite, is also appropriate at this rite.

The circle is closed in the manner discussed in chapter seven. The after-ritual activities usually center on feasting. After all, this is a harvest ritual.

A Ritual for the Autumn Equinox

Timing: There is no best time to perform this ritual.

Preparation: An additional altar, the harvest altar, should be placed in the center of the circle. If necessary, place the main altar a bit to the east and the harvest altar a bit to the west. The harvest altar should be low enough to the ground so that one can sit on the ground and feel comfortable eating at the table. If a table is not available, spread a cloth on the ground.

A blindfold, cauldron, or tub of water, apples for everyone in attendance, and a knife, possibly the working knife, for cutting the apples should be placed close to the harvest altar. Drums and noisemakers are very appropriate at this rite. Extra noisemakers such as hardwood sticks and rattles should be placed on the harvest altar. Guests should be encouraged to bring gourds to decorate the altar. These gourds should be dried and turned into rattles for next year's celebration.

A crown for the King of the Harvest should be placed on the God half of the altar. A second crown similar to the King's should be placed on the Goddess half of the altar for the Queen.

Food and drink, also on the harvest altar, should be plentiful. Everyone who attends this rite should make an effort to bring a canned or nonperishable food item which will be collected, blessed, and given to a needy member of the group or local shelter.

The Ritual: The temple is erected as discussed in chapter 7, except the symbolic Great Rite is not performed at this point.

Priestess: "This is a time of balance. It is a time when the day and night are in balance."

Priest: "This is a time when the light is replaced by darkness. We enter a time when the day grows shorter and the night grows longer."

Priestess: "This is the second harvest. Our table is full, but we need a Queen of the Harvest."

The Priestess leads the women to the apples and water. The Priest starts a slow beat for the drummers and hands out the noisemakers. The Priestess fills the water with the apples. She marks one of the apples by cutting away a half-inch slice in its skin. The women are blindfolded one at a time. They bob for apples until the marked apple is retrieved as the men entertain with drumming, song, and chants. It is appropriate for each woman to be limited to a minute or two. Decrease the number of apples in the water if you want to make things go quicker. Small apples are easier to catch in the mouth. If an unmarked apple is caught, it is eaten. If no one seems to be able to snag an apple with their mouth, let them use their hands. Once the Priestess finds a winner, she sends the winner to pridefully saunter past the men, moving clockwise around the circle to show off the apple. She is the Queen of the Harvest.

Priest: "This is the second harvest. Our table is full, but we need a King of the Harvest."

The Priest leads the men to the apples and water. The Priest marks a second apple the way the Priestess marked the first. The men are blindfolded one at a time. They bob for apples until the marked apple is retrieved. As they do, the Priestess leads the women in entertaining with drumming, song, and chants, which continues as it did when the women were bobbing for apples until there is a winner. The winner is sent to strut past the women, moving clockwise around the circle to show off the apple. He is the King of the Harvest.

The Priestess then crowns the King of the Harvest and the Priest crowns the Queen. For the rest of this rite, the Queen acts as Priestess and the King as the Priest. The Priest and Priestess should guide them if they are not completely familiar with the rite. The group is gathered around the harvest altar and the King and Queen perform the symbolic Great Rite over the harvest altar. The feast begins.

During the feast, the cans and nonperishable food are collected and placed on the harvest altar. Drumming, singing, and chanting are more than welcome. The games from the Bealtaine ritual are also welcome, as are other simple games, during this rite.

When the King and Queen feel it is time to end the feast, they gather all the participants back into their places in the circle. An apple is given to everyone in attendance with the assurance that the revelry does not have to stop. The circle is closed in the manner discussed in chapter 7, except that the closing is conducted by the King and Queen of the Harvest with the help and direction of the Priest and Priestess. This helps to train other group members.

A Final Word

Today, Wicca is almost entrenched in American culture. However, the world is not static. The religious freedom that we now enjoy can be taken away. It was not that long ago that the rights guaranteed under the Constitution of this great nation were thought to apply to only white men. Even today, women and minorities struggle for equal rights.

If we do not want to relive history, we will do well to remember it. In October of 1996, I was interviewed by a local newspaper. The reporter was addressing the issue of Halloween being celebrated in the public school systems. The matter was a hot issue in the press because several Christian organizations were insisting that it be banned because it was a Pagan holiday. As such, the Christian organization felt its celebration had no place in the schools of a Christian nation. The reporter was disappointed to find that I agreed that it should not be celebrated in the school system. It was one of the first times that I can remember agreeing with the far right. I responded as I did because I am a strict supporter of the separation between Church and

181

State. Halloween (most often called Samhain by Neo-Pagans) has no place in public schools. Christmas, Easter, and all other religious celebrations should not be commemorated within state-funded organizations. It doesn't matter who is being governed. It is only possible to experience religious freedom when those who govern have no involvement with the religion of those being governed.

Since my introduction to Wicca in 1979, and even more since I opened my Neo-Pagan shop in 1993, I have heard warnings of the return of the Burning Times (the Great Darkness or the Inquisition). In the United States, such a return to the darkness is highly unlikely without constitutional changes. In this country, the First Amendment guarantees us the right to freedom of religion. If you find yourself persecuted due to your religious beliefs, there are specific legal actions available. If monotheists of the far right break into your home with the intention of burning you at the stake, you have every legal right to defend yourself.

Wiccans do not need to be pacifists. Although the Wiccan Rede states, "an it harm none, do what thou will," this does not instruct the Wiccan not to do harm. This simply states that if it harms none and you want to do it, then don't question the action. The implication to this portion of the Rede is, if your action will cause harm, consider the action before taking it. A popular belief is that the second amendment enforces the first.

If our nation truly honors these two monumental principles, that there should remain a separation between Church and State and that each individual has the right to freedom of religion, then the darkness cannot return. There is a strong tendency for those on deeply spiritual paths to avoid taking an active role in politics. I am personally fond of the bumper sticker that reads "Religious groups should stay out of politics or be taxed." The reality of the matter is that those who are not willing to fight for freedom will become enslaved. Our culture has come a long way, but freedom is a living and growing thing. If we nurture it, it will grow. If we neglect it, it will wilt. If we ignore it entirely, take it for granted, it will die.

Blessed be and live free.

Appendix A: References

Note: References and associations tend to change from culture to culture. These are the associations that have worked well for my household and for myself.

Quarter Associations

Association	East	South	West	North
Element	Air	Fire	Water	Earth
Part of being	Breath	Soul/Spirit	Blood	Body
State	Gas	Energy	Liquid	Solid
Condition	Hot/Moist	Hot/Dry	Cold/Moist	Cold/Dry
Color	Yellow	Red	Blue	Green
Gender	Male	Male	Female	Female
Tool	Censer	Athame	Chalice	Pentacle
Complement	North	West	South	East
Moon cycle	New moon	Waxing quarter	Full moon	Waning quarter
Sun cycle	Spring Equinox	Summer Solstice	Autumn Equinox	Winter Solstice
Time of day	Sunrise	Midday	Sundown	Midnight
Primary planet	Mercury	Sun	Moon	Venus
Secondary planet	Uranus	Mars	Jupiter	Saturn
Primary flower	Lavender	Rose geranium	Rose	Patchouly
Primary jewel	Topaz	Fire opal	Aquamarine	Emerald
Other minerals	Aventurine	Ruby	Sapphire	Malachite
	Mika	Bloodstone	Moonstone	Peridot
Metals	Mercury	Gold	Aquamarine	Lead

185

Zodiac Associations

Zodiac Sign	Dates	Ruling Planet	Element	Associated Colors
Aquarius	Jan. 20–Feb. 18	Saturn/Uranus	Air	Blue and green
Aries	Mar. 21–Apr. 19	Mars	Fire	Pink, red, and white
Cancer	June 21–July 22	Moon	Water	Brown, green, and white
Capricorn	Dec. 22–Jan. 19	Saturn	Earth	Black, brown, and red
Gemini	May 21–June 20	Gemini	Air	Blue, red, and yellow
Leo	July 23–Aug. 22	Sun	Fire	Green, red, and yellow
Libra	Sept. 23–Oct. 22	Venus	Air	Black, blue, and yellow
Pisces	Feb. 19–Mar. 20	Jupiter/Neptune	Water	Green and white
Sagittarius	Nov. 22–Dec. 21	Jupiter	Fire	Purple, red, and yellow
Scorpio	Oct. 23–Nov. 21	Mars	Water	Black, brown, and red
Taurus	Apr. 20–May 20	Venus	Earth	Green, red, and yellow
Virgo	Aug. 23–Sept. 22	Mercury	Earth	Black, gray, and yellow

Zodiac Associations of Herbs and Minerals

Zodiac Sign	Some of the Associated Herbs	Some of the Associated Minerals
Aquarius	Acacia, lavender, mace, and pine	Garnet, turquoise, hawkeye
Aries	Allspice, cinnamon, clove, and peppermint	Red jasper, carnelian, bloodstone
Cancer	Eucalyptus, jasmine, lemon, and rose	Emerald, chrysoprase, green aventurine
Capricorn	Magnolia, oakmoss, vervain, and Vetivert	Onyx, cat's eye, ruby
Gemini	Almond, anise, dill, and lavender	Citrine, agate, tiger's eye
Leo	Nutmeg, orange, rosemary, and sandalwood	Citrine, onyx, quartz crystal
Libra	Catnip, lilac, mugwort, and thyme	Smoky quartz, citrine, chrysolite
Pisces	Anise, gardenia, lemon, and sarsaparilla	Amethyst
Sagittarius	Carnation, honeysuckle, sage, and sassafras	Chalcedony, topaz
Scorpio	Basil, cumin, ginger, and violet	Red carnelian, aquamarine
Taurus	Cardamom, lilac, patchouly, and vanilla	Rose quartz, sapphire
Virgo	Cypress, dill, fennel, and lily	Citrine, carnelian

Mineral Associations With the Months
of the Year

Month of the Year	*Some of the Associated Minerals*
January	Garnet and rose quartz
February	Amethyst and onyx
March	Aquamarine and bloodstone
April	Diamond and sapphire
May	Emerald and chrysoprase
June	Pearl and moonstone
July	Ruby, carnelian, onyx, and turquoise
August	Peridot, aventurine, and sardonyx
September	Sapphire, lapis, and chrysolite
October	Opal, tourmaline, and beryl
November	Topaz and tiger's eye
December	Turquoise, zircon, and ruby

Essential Oil Associations

Essential Oils	*Element*	*Planet*	*Brief Magickal Associations*
Bay	Fire	Sun	Enhances psychic abilities, divination, purification
Benzoin	Air	Mercury	Increases physical, cognitive, and magickal energy
Bergamot	Fire	Sun	Induces sleep, peace, and happiness
Black pepper	Fire	Mars	Encourages alertness and physical energy
Camphor	Water	Moon	Increases physical energy, celibacy, purification
Cedar	Fire	Sun	Enhances self-control, promotes spirituality
Cypress	Earth	Saturn	Speeds healing, lessens grief
Eucalyptus	Air	Mercury	Speeds healing, purifies
Frankincense	Air	Sun	Promotes meditation and spirituality; also for protection

Essential Oils	*Element*	*Planet*	*Brief Magickal Associations*
Geranium	Water	Venus	Promotes happiness, wards off negative energy (protection)
Ginger	Fire	Mars	Enhances magickal and physical energy, draws love and money
Hyssop	Fire	Jupiter	Enhances the conscious mind; also for purification
Juniper	Fire	Sun	Promotes healing; also for protection and purification
Lavender	Air	Mercury	Promotes sleep and dreams; also for love and health
Lemon	Water	Moon	Enhances physical energy, promotes healing and health
Lemon balm	Air	Jupiter	Attracts prosperity, promotes peace and purification
Lemon grass	Air	Mercury	Promotes psychic awareness
Lime	Fire	Sun	Enhances psychic energy; also for protection and purification
Myrrh	Water	Saturn	Promotes meditation and spirituality, promotes healing
Orange	Fire	Sun	Enhances physical and magickal energy
Patchouly	Earth	Saturn	Attracts women, increases physical and sexual energy
Peppermint	Air	Mercury	Enhances conscious thought; also for purification
Pine	Air	Mars	Enhances physical and magickal energy, attracts prosperity
Sandalwood	Water	Moon	Promotes meditation and spirituality, healing and sex
Vanilla	Water	Venus	Enhances physical and magickal energy; attracts men
Vetivert	Earth	Venus	Draws money and wealth; also for protection
Ylang-Ylang	Water	Venus	Promotes love and peace; increases sexual desire

Appendix B: Resources

Supply Resource Directory

When I first became interested in the Craft, finding a shop that offered the supplies I desired was next to impossible. I lived in South Bend, Indiana, at the time. When finances and need met each other, friends and I would take the south shore train line into Chicago and spend the day hiking the city in search of supplies. At one shop we'd find herbs and oils. The next shop might yield candles and incense. Books were most often found under dust on the bottom shelf in the back corner of mainstream bookstores. Today, shops aimed directly at the Neo-Pagan and Wiccan community are popping up everywhere. When one considers the meaning of the word *"occult"* is hidden, it is surprising to find a listing for occult in the Yellow Pages. If your phone book has no such listings, check under books and religious supplies. It is always preferable to be able to see, hold, smell, feel, and sometimes taste merchandise before you purchase it, but if you are forced to use mail order, there are some truly reputable suppliers listed at the end of this directory.

Tools

Coins are often used in conjunction with bills or by themselves because they are a more tangible expression of worth than paper. Silver and gold coins are available in most areas. Check coin and collectable shops. I prefer to use coins that have come into my store's register by chance. They seem to work best and have acquired the most meaning.

Essential oils are the essence of a plant. Beware of blended or synthetic oils. Blended oils are often made from true essentials, but are then cut with less expensive filler oils. Synthetic oils contain none of the plant material and generally smell like plastic when burned. True essentials are best found at local herb stores, some health food shops, and magickal suppliers.

Herbs are available at many natural food, health, and grocery stores. Some of the more esoteric herbs, such as mandrake and high john can only be found at specialty shops. Look in the Yellow Pages under herbs or botanicals.

Image candles are available at almost any Neo-Pagan and magick-oriented shop. They come in a variety of colors, most often green, red, pink, black, and white. If you have trouble finding them, you can purchase wedding candles (bride and groom images) at wedding supply shops. To make individual candles, the couple can be easily separated using a warm knife.

Poppets are dolls, statues, or other images designed to represent a specific person. These are most often called Voodoo dolls, however, the use of such devices is much more widespread than only Voodoo. They can be purchased at many occult/magick shops, but it is best to make them yourself.

Semiprecious minerals can be found in many New Age, Pagan, and gift shops. If you can't find what you are looking for, check the Yellow Pages for rock shops and lapidary supplies. Don't let the word precious scare you. Most items are available as low-cost tumbles.

Sachets are fabric bags. They can be purchased at most gift stores, many jewelry stores, and at herb shops. You can make a simple sachet by cutting a piece of fabric into the needed size, placing what it will hold into the center, and then drawing the sides up to a central point where it can be tied with a ribbon.

Voodoo doll—See Poppet.

Mail Order Supplies

This is only a tiny list of what is available. For a much more complete listing, please see *The Wicca Source Book*, by Gerina Dunwich (published by Carol Publishing Group, ISBN 0-8065-2027-2 [pbk.]). With the ISBN, even mainstream bookstores can order it for you.

Azure Green and Abyss Distribution
48 Chester Road W.F.M.
Chester, MA 01011
Phone: (413) 623-2155; Fax: (413) 623-2156

The business that is now Azure Green and Abyss Distribution started with a retail location and grew into a mail order business unlike any other. Nestled on the verge of the Berkshire Mountains in Massachusetts, the business has become a small village. While I have yet to meet Adair (the primary owner), during a family member's trip through Massachusetts, he welcomed her as if she were his family. These are good people.

Circle Network News
P.O. Box 219
Mt. Horeb, WI 53572
Voice Mail: (608) 924-2216

Circle Sanctuary is the publisher of the quarterly Neo-Pagan journal *Circle Network News*. They also publish a networking/retail directory, *Circle Guide to Pagan Groups*. This is an excellent source book of Pagan-oriented mail order and retail stores.

Llewellyn Worldwide and Llewellyn New Worlds
P.O. Box 64383
St. Paul, MN 55164
Phone: (800) 844-6666

Llewellyn Worldwide is the publisher of *Llewellyn New Worlds of Mind and Spirit*. This magazine/catalog features a reader's forum, horoscope, book reviews, and a New Age marketplace section where you will find listings for numerous mail order businesses. Beware! Like most periodicals, Llewellyn is not responsible for the claims made by their advertisers.

Salem West
1209 North High St.
Columbus, OH 43201
Phone: (614) 421-7557; Fax: (614) 326-0470
Web site: http://www.neopagan.com

Owned by yours truly, Salem West prides itself on direct
involvement with today's authors and products produced by them
or in accordance with their instructions. In addition to our retail
location, Salem West has strong involvement in the arts and one-
of-a-kind creations. We maintain a two-thousand-square-foot stu-
dio and have plans to open a full-scale gallery. Our catalog is free
and is shipped with the latest information on the annual Real
Witches' Ball.

Bibliography

Buckland, Raymond. *Buckland's Complete Book of Witchcraft*. St. Paul: Llewellyn Publications, 1997.

———. *Practical Color Magick*. St. Paul: Llewellyn Publications, 1994.

Budapest, Zsuzsanna. *The Grandmother of Time*. San Francisco: HarperCollins Publishing, 1979.

Cunningham, Scott. *Wicca: A Guide for the Solitary Practitioner*. St. Paul: Llewellyn Publications, 1978.

———. *Magical Aromatherapy*. St. Paul: Llewellyn Publications, 1996.

Davidson, H. R. *Gods and Myths of Northern Europe*. London: Penguin Books, 1964.

Farrar, Stewart. *What Witches Do*. Custer, WA: Phoenix Publishing, 1995.

Farrar, Janet and Stewart. *Eight Sabbats for Witches*. Custer, WA: Phoenix Publishing, 1981.

———. *The Witches' God*. Custer, WA: Phoenix Publishing, 1989.

———. *The Witches' Goddess*. Custer, WA: Phoenix Publishing, 1995.

Guerber, H. A. *Myths of the Norsemen*. New York: Dover Publications, 1929.

Liddell, W. E. *The Pickingill Papers*. United Kingdom: Capall Bann Publishing, 1994.

McCoy, Edain. *The Sabbats*. St. Paul: Lewellyn Publications, 1996.

Murray, Margaret. *The Witch Cult in Western Europe*. Oxford, England: Oxford Paperbacks, 1962.

O'Hara, Gwydion. *Moonlore*. St. Paul: Llewellyn Publications, 1996.
————. *Sunlore*. St. Paul: Llewellyn Publications, 1997.
Sanders, Alex. *The Alex Sanders Lectures*. New York: Magickal Childe Publishing, 1984.
Telesco, Patricia. *Seasons of the Sun*. York Beach, ME: Samuel Weiser, 1996.
Wendell, Leilah. *Encounters With Death*. New Orleans, LA: West Gate Press, 1996.